Kamau Brathwaite ar

Curwen Best

Kamau Brathwaite and Christopher Okigbo

Art, Politics, and the Music of Ritual

PETER LANG
Bern · Berlin · Bruxelles · Frankfurt am Main · New York · Oxford · Wien

Bibliographic information published by Die Deutsche Bibliothek
Die Deutsche Bibliothek lists this publication in the Deutsche Nationalbibliografie; detailed bibliographic data is available on the Internet at ‹http://dnb.ddb.de›.

British Library Cataloguing-in-Publication Data:
A catalogue record for this book is available from The British Library, Great Britain

Library of Congress Cataloging-in-Publication Data

Best, Curwen.
Kamau Brathwaite and Christopher Okigbo : art, politics, and the music of ritual / Curwen Best.
p. cm.
Includes bibliographical references.
ISBN 978-3-03911-716-1 (alk. paper)
1. Brathwaite, Kamau, 1930–Criticism and interpretation. 2. Okigbo, Christopher, 1932-1967–Criticism and interpretation. 3. Literature, Comparative–Caribbean (English) and Nigerian (English) 4. Literature, Comparative–Nigerian (English) and Caribbean (English) 5. Caribbean Area–In literature. 6. Nigeria–In literature. I. Title.
PR9230.9.B68Z53 2009
811'.54–dc22

2009005123

The painting on the book cover is "Tribute" by Edmund Gill. It is a tribute to the nameless woodcarvers of Africa, especially the Bamina (Bambara) people of Mali.

Cover design: Eva Rolli, Peter Lang AG

ISBN 978-3-03911-716-1

Hochfeldstrasse 32, Postfach 746, CH-3000 Bern 9, Switzerland
info@peterlang.com, www.peterlang.com, www.peterlang.net

Printed in Germany

To my wife, Charmaine,
and to our little son Christopher-Chars

Table of Contents

Acknowledgements

To God for guidance, strength and ability. To the publishers, especially Daniela Christen for her insight and professionalism. To Edmund Gill for permission to reproduce his painting "Tribute" on the front cover. To the family circle for their unending support. Most of all, to the love of my life, my wife, Charmaine whose love, strength and courage inspired me to take this project through. To Christopher-Chars for keeping us alert and reassuring us that God's plan is sure.

Brathwaite and Okigbo in Overview

Many years ago Kamau Brathwaite made the statement that Barbadians are the most Igbo-like of all the Caribbean peoples. This statement was in some respect a sociological perception. Yes, he did suggest that the Barbadian slave could have been Igbo, given the extent of their passion for religion and democracy: but the statement was made to provoke academics, cultural workers, critics, and researchers, whom he seemed to be challenging to make crosscultural connections at various levels and by way of a range of analyses. His statement therefore seemed a challenge to re-engage and renew a type of scholarship that has been a significant thread in the work of Africanists and Caribbeanists. Other critics and activists have also expressed the wish for more comparative work that links the Caribbean to Africa: for example, the Kenyan Ngugi wa Thiong'o has expressed his concern about current opportunities for increasing Caribbean Studies within African institutions:

> On looking back I am amazed by our utter neglect of Caribbean Studies in our Departments of Literature. How can we ignore the most exciting literary outbursts in the world today? We forget, or have been made to forget by our literary midwives from Britain, that the West Indies has been very formative in Africa's political and literary consciousness.[1]

Both Brathwaite and Okigbo were born into societies controlled externally and by the same political master: England. Despite the cultural and other differences between their homelands (Nigeria and Barbados), their experiences as young citizens in

1 Ngugi wa Thiong'o, *Homecoming* (London: Heinemann, 1972) 81.

the pre-Independence period were significantly shaped by the impact of colonial structures on the body politic and on social, cultural, and religious life. Their societies were to some degree still suffering under the weight of colonial expansionism, but change seemed imminent. This pre-Independence period saw the confrontation of systems of belief and knowledge which anticipated the turmoil that would erupt across much of Africa and the Caribbean in the 1930s and beyond.

Okigbo and Brathwaite can said to have emerged as artists at the moment of incipient maturation of their regional literatures: thus their particular function and literary contribution is integral to understanding the kinds of tensions at play within their societies just before and just after the formal granting of Independence to their respective nations, and in assessing their work one cannot but measure their response to the range of issues that confronted their societies as they wrestled with questions of identity, nationalism, sovereignty, liberation, and power. These two artists are in some respect representative of their colleagues: I do not claim that they are the only artists of the period whose work can be held up in this way, but rather that they are crucial components of the dynamics at work within their nations and region. A general reading of criticism and comment, academic or otherwise, shows us how centrally placed they are. Each writer's work is like a critical artistic centrepiece which can be observed, examined, and judged to gain a better understanding of what West African and West Indian poetry is all about, and to come to a fuller awareness of the dynamic possibilities within these two traditions.

In addition to their treatment of similar themes in the realms of history, tradition, and the system (political and educational), spirituality is also central to their work, and this book pays significant attention to their spiritual and artistic quest. It can be said that their work is defined by an ongoing concern with the spiritual odyssey and that this journey is underscored by an equally significant artistic process where form, style, and language are constantly foregrounded. Both Okigbo and Brathwaite write with a keen awareness of and a heavy reliance upon music, musicality, and orality, and it can even be argued that their poems are meant primarily for the ear, and that the printed page does not offer full access to and appreciation of their dynamic creations. Since they have produced poetry that can be regarded as indigenous, universal, formulaic, and experimental, there are many points of tension within their work. If they display similarities, they are also different in some respects. If Okigbo's work undergoes a process of indigenization by the end of the collection *Labyrinths*, Brathwaite's work under consideration here seems to go in the opposite direction by the time we reach *X/Self*. *X/Self* is about Barbadian and Caribbean concerns, but its frame of reference is much broader. While Brathwaite's driving motivation is to come to terms with African–Caribbean and African–New World culture over a sustained period, Okigbo's initial emphasis is on understanding complex truths about the individual and the wider universe. In his latter days he was motivated by the desire to reconcile the conflict between art and politics.

This book responds to the imbalance in the quantity of material produced by the two poets by focusing mainly on Brathwaite's earlier widely published work and hardly going beyond the second trilogy of poems (*Mother Poem, Sun Poem,* and *X/Self*). The text entitled *Labyrinths, with Path of Thunder* (first published by Heinemann in 1971) is the main text used for the appraisal of Christopher Okigbo's poetry. These works by the two authors reflect their responses to the social, cultural, artistic, and political concerns of the Independence era.

This study seeks to create a greater interest in the area of cross-cultural poetics. It considers aspects of the historical link between two regions that have been substantially affected by the process of colonialism. Our concern with history and tradition is not intended to deify more traditional culture while casting doubt on the more contemporary. Rather, this book wants to examine the nature of colonialism's impact on the social, political, cultural, and spiritual life of the two authors and regions under consideration. The two poets through their creative work offer an opportunity for conducting such an examination, and this close scrutiny represents a vital intervention in an area of relative critical void. I am not aware of the publication of a study of this kind that juxtaposes the work of these two major poets.

Since this study is literary and cultural rather than sociological, thematic concerns are only one part of its focus; it is also interested in the areas of language, style, and technique. Especially in this regard, the whole concern of the link with history/tradition resurfaces to question the modern artist's role in present-day society: why he speaks, to whom, and on whose behalf.

This is a comparative work. It should be made clear, however, that the discussion throughout does not seek to hinge Brathwaite to Okigbo and vice versa at every moment. This is not that kind of comparative work. This book recognizes that these two authors also exist separately in the sphere of academic criticism. This is to say that there is a body of criticism and knowledge surrounding each writer; and one of this book's secondary objectives is to engage with that criticism, while ultimately fleshing out a more complete picture of who the two writers are and what their work represents. The initial chapters of the book give the historical, social, cultural, spiritual, and political context of the writers, as well as sketching their biography: thereafter the discussion concerns itself with examining their individual artistic responses to their experiences. The investigation of these responses is arranged by assigning individual chapters to each author and/or a specific work or (in most cases) works. So while there is some side-by-side comparison within chapters, the sequential arrangement of chapters around central issues also allows for a much more panoramic perspective: there are many more issues treated within this work.

CHAPTER 1

Grounding: Background, Context, and Scope

This chapter is an attempt to add contextual depth to this book. Along with the subsequent chapter on language and culture this one helps to lay the foundation for a close examination of the contribution of these major national, regional, and international poets. The brief descriptive history presented here is meant primarily to serve as a basis for understanding socio-political and cultural mores within both societies (Nigeria and Barbados). It is hoped that the descriptions will enhance and crystallize the reader's perception of these writers. In addition, this chapter identifies each writer's genesis within his respective literary tradition and places him in relation to his contemporaries. Some attention is paid to the personal lives of both poets, in as much as this information contributes to our understanding of the work under consideration. The inherent distinctions between their regions and cultures must perforce be reflected within their literature; hence some attention is given to this difference and its implications for the critic who attempts a comparative study of this kind.

Some of the information presented in this chapter will no doubt resurface in other chapters. Indeed, this chapter does not cover all facets of the history and life and times of these artists, but other sections of this work will supply some of the gaps that emerge within this compressed overview.

Emphasis in this chapter is placed on the broader parameters into which Okigbo and Brathwaite fit: African – more precisely West African – literature, and West Indian literature. This chapter is not concerned with creating definitions of these literatures, but proceeds upon the assumption that these boundaries can be imagined, if not firmly established. Given its desire to provide a context for the major discussion that follows it, this chapter sacrifices some depth of analysis in favour of breadth of coverage. It moves from a generalized perspective of literature and literatures to a more specialized scrutiny of Brathwaite and Okigbo. The heavy reliance on and reference to Afro-West Indian writing is deliberate, since the focus of this study leads to such a slant, while not totally ignoring other influences.

By the end of this introductory chapter, then, the uninitiated should possess a better understanding of not only Nigerian and West Indian cultures and literatures, but also of the challenges posed to this kind of extended critical study.

1. A Brief History

The phenomenon of colonial domination is well known to the peoples of Africa and the West Indies, and the façades of these contemporary societies have been shaped by it. It was the capitalist thirst for money and power that fuelled European expansionism, ultimately forcing the movement of peoples of Africa to the Caribbean.

1.1 Nigeria

History texts speak of attempts at conquest and domination and about Nigeria having come under some occupation prior to the incursion of the British. Coleman refers to 'external influence' from the grand medieval kingdoms of the western Sahara –

Ghana, Melle, and Songhai.[1] But no colonial influence would be so uniformly pervasive and influential as that of the British. This is not to suggest that the British had easily overrun and colonized this vast territory. As late as 1900 the British had not conquered all the areas of the Eastern Provinces, and it was not until 1918 that they were able to bring all of Igboland under effective British administration. The tenacity of this latter region would prove to be a challenge to the central administration and its allies during the Igbo secession struggle called the Biafran War (1967–1970).

The six years commencing 1906 witnessed a transformation within many aspects of Nigerian life; Nigeria was impacted upon as at no other time.[2] During the post-World War One period and up to 1960 there was a second phase of change, towards nationalism. But it was in this first pre-World War One period that Nigerian society was changed most drastically. A new economic world was born, along with new methods of administration and justice. The role of missionaries had been established, there was a surge of Christian doctrinal teaching, and education in Western ways of life bombarded local traditional values which had been in place for generations. Nigeria was no more its old self, and this transformation process came to influence those born in the 1930s such as Christopher Okigbo.

The late 1930s and 1940s witnessed a counterswing towards nationalism, a mood which had taken over much of the continent as a result of universal economic, political, and social factors. The effects were being felt in Nigeria, but never resulted in an all-pervasive union because there had always been political tensions between the northern zone and the south and demarcations between the Yoruba, Hausa, Muslims, and Igbos. These divisions gave rise to numerous factional squabbles and

1 James Coleman, *Nigeria; A Background of Nationalism* (Berkeley: University of California Press, 1971) 36.

2 Michael Crowder, *The Story of Nigeria* (London: Faber, 1978) 189.

several declarations of states of emergency; so that when Independence came in November 1960, euphoric outbursts merely obfuscated the impending breakdown in administration, which many had perceived as inevitable: complaints over politicians' 'corruption' and 'profligacy' were already being voiced by the early 1960s.[3] North–South tensions persisted over the question of the proportion of representatives in the federal parliament; there were violent demonstrations against the Anglo-Nigerian Defence Pact; and friction between the Action Group and federal government over the creation of a Mid-West Region resulted in a state of emergency being declared in 1962 and Obafemi Awolowo and his supporters being arrested. A second general strike took place in 1964. All these were a prelude to the civil war of 1967 in which Christopher Okigbo was a casualty.

1.2 Barbados

Britain's dealings with the West Indian territory of Barbados began as early as the 1620s, a monument in honour of King James I being erected in 1627. The year 1639 saw the selection of a number of burgesses; this was the first parliament. Whereas Nigeria had posed particular problems for potential colonizers, Barbados had presented very few. Topographical differences would be a major factor in Nigeria, which was much vaster and more heavily populated, and had numerous social groupings of clan-like peoples of distinctive habits and languages, all of which contributed to Britain's administrative perplexities over many years. Barbados, on the other hand, an island of just 166 square miles and with smaller homogenous groupings, could hardly have posed the kinds of problems encountered in Nigeria. After the native Amerindian population was driven

3 Crowder, *The Story of Nigeria* 260.

out or killed off, the conquerors were able to subdue and retain the small island for centuries.

It was during the slave trade that Africa and the West Indies came into constant contact, when slaves were transported thither across the Atlantic from Africa's west coast. The potent impact that Britain inflicted upon Nigeria's entire body social was redoubled in the case of Barbados, the island having remained in British hands throughout and never falling to other colonial masters. Nigeria's six years of transformation through social, political, economic, and psychological bombardment was redoubled in Barbados over the centuries of British rule. The British Empire left an indelible mark on the major sectors and areas of Barbadian life including education, religion, and the political and social sector: but perhaps its greatest impact was made on the Barbadian psyche. So great would be the influence of the British that despite the formal granting of Independence in 1966, Barbados would be referred to, even today, as 'Little England'.

2. A Perception of West African Verse: Depth of Written Verse

When Chinweizu made the important suggestion that scholarship would do well to exhume Africa's classical traditions and clarify and disseminate them so that they could be useful to us today, he was responding to a view that there was no such thing as literature in west Africa prior to the arrival of the Europeans. To suggest that West African literature (and thus West African writing) began (and in English) in the eighteenth century,[4] a period of humanitarianism, through Africa's contact with Britain's publishing houses and with such works as Ignatius Sancho's published letters, Ottobah Cugoano's *Thoughts and Sentiments on the Evil and Wicked Traffic of the Slavery and Commerce of the Human Species, Humbly Submitted to the Inhabitants of Great Britain* (1787), and Equiano's *Interesting Narrative of the Life of Ouladah Equiano or Gustavus Vassa, the African* is to underestimate the depth of autonomy within African literature/writing.

Although the latter half of the twentieth century witnessed a greater awareness of Africa's potential, there are still many people who question the legitimacy and authenticity of African literature. Thus, Tutuola's *The Palm-Wine Drinkard* is not classified under the category of novel, nor is it accorded the status of African folk tale. Rather, it is a 'ghost novel', a fantasy, and an allegory. Some creative African writing is therefore treated as a curiosity or aberration, something to be looked upon with condescending indulgence. An article that appeared back in 1960 best demonstrates the supercilious attitude of some Western criticism of that period. Keith Waterhouse comments on the 'simplicity of style' of Achebe's works (more specifically *No Longer at Ease*), and then goes on to assert: 'later when the chronicles of change are more or less complete, some very fortunate writers indeed will be able to fill the framework in, wallowing in the new luxuries of characterization, motivation, depth, psychology and all the rest of it.'[5] Here the impression is conveyed that this and similar works of the period constitute the genesis of African literature in the broadest sense, and that when the 'chronicles' of change are complete Africa can expect

4 Too many criticisms of West African literature have tended to create the impression (if not by direct statement) that West African literature/writing came about purely through British influence. See Abiola Irele in 'The Criticism of Modern African Literature', *Perspectives on African Literature*, ed. Christopher Heywood (London: Heinemann, 1971) 10.

5 Keith Waterhouse, *New Statesman* Lx 17 (1960): 398.

a new body of work made up of writings steeped in the Western mode and revealed through *its* idiom. Surprisingly, although Tutuola's work operates in the supranatural and natural worlds, and works like Achebe's are comparatively mundane and palpable, they are often undifferentiated in some criticism of the period, and categorized as being juvenile. This is the case with some critics who have read, 'understood', and greatly appreciated works like *Faust/Faustus* (in its many treatments) for their psychology, when they also consist of a journey between worlds and an examination of the interplay between life and death and the protagonist's several responses.[6] This leads vicariously to man's (the reader's) catharsis through the encounter.[7] Still, Marlowe's *Doctor Faustus* is not a ghost play.[8]

In *Perspectives on African Literature* Lalage Brown examines writing from 1769 and seems to suggest that when Africans first started to write it was in English.[9] But since the West Indian Francis Williams (b. 1700) was capable of writing in Latin, we must look for an even longer African legacy of writing.[10] Two centuries earlier the East African Juan Latino had been writing

6 Smeed takes a compelling look into the origin and the development of the Faust myth/archetype, and notes that Marlowe's Faust is 'psychologically convincing'. See J. Smeed, *Faust In Literature* (London: Oxford University Press, 1975) 5.

7 Where Smeed comments about the universal truth of all subsequent treatments of Faust, this is also captured in Spies's version where he notes that the story is told as 'a fearful warning'.

8 This is not an attempt to squarely categorize Marlowe's *Faustus* with Tutuola's *The Palm-Wine Drinkard,* since they are quite distinct in many aspects, especially with regard to style and structure. But the two works are similar to the extent that they use the supernatural to make a profound statement to humankind.

9 Lalage Brown, 'The Development of African Prose writing in English: A Perspective', *Perspectives on African Literature,* ed. Christopher Heywood (London: Heinemann, 1971) 33–34.

10 Though Latin was the literary dominant language, subsequently to be replaced by English, it should be remembered that English was not the primary language for a writer in Africa.

plays and verse in Latin, and though very much a Spaniard by residence and perhaps also in intention (since much of his writing was dedicated to the monarchy and papacy, for example his *Epigrammatum Liber* in honour of the birth of Prince Ferdinand), his 'preoccupation with panegyrics might in some measure' have been a result of his African origin, as Dathorne suggests.[11] Given the vibrant function of praise poetry throughout the continent (Finnegan speaks of the Muslim festivals of Eid-ul-Fitr and Eid-ul-Kabir, where the king's name is extolled)[12] and given Latino's impressionistic twelve years within such a culture, there can be little doubt that there was indeed an influence. Although it is a fact that he became a devout Catholic in Spain, one also knows that the retention and assimilation of old practices is not unheard of in the area of religious conversion. In fact, Latino consciously deals with this theme/idea in *Epigrammatum Liber* where he almost insists that 'when Philip met the Ethiopian he taught him about Christ verbally / Christ sent a disciple to an Ethiopian.'[13] We learn that Philip left, and eventually so did the Eunuch of Ethiopia, the latter with a new philosophy and perhaps with a new religion as well, but physiologically still a eunuch, and ultimately still Black.[14] Latino's life writing (and even its style) is a restatement of this point.

In the nineteenth century persons like one Pilane, though not writing in Latin but in his native southern African, Tswana, was echoing Latino's style and attitude of exalted praise, but also drawing from the local:

11 O. R. Dathorne, *The Black Mind* (Minneapolis: University of Minnesota Press, 1974) 69.

12 Ruth Finnegan, *Oral Literature in Africa* (Nairobi: Oxford University Press, 1970) 120.

13 Edward Long, *The History of Jamaica* (London: For T. Lowndes, 1774) 476.

14 *Holy Bible,* King James version 'Acts of the Apostles' (Tennessee: Crusade Bible Publishers Inc., 1977) Chapter 8 vs. 39.

I am Pilane the war-monger
the scratcher, companion of Motswasejane ...
Pilane is a rock of ironstone
he is a slippery rock, Pilane,
those who touch him will lose their fingers
Mabine touched him and lost his fingers.[15]

And well into the twentieth century, even though in a modified form, the traditional motifs of the panegyric – metaphorical comparison, allusion, adulatory address, and parallelism – are still evident in African poetry. This latter feature is epitomized in Okara's verse:

Letlhola hommaeno gobeolwa
Letlhola bommaneo golala balla

(you foredoom your mothers to mourn
you foredoom your mothers to weep all night)

Moleti amatlotta molebeledi
wamarope abatho modisa
wsope lagammaagwe

(Watchman of derelict homes,
caretaker of people's ruins
guardian of his mother's deserted house)[16]

The early influence of Swahili in northern Africa provides another example of non-European input within African writings. It is known that a corpus of written verse in Swahili was produced in the coastal towns of East Africa as early as the eighteenth century.[17] This has a lexical form extraneous to the world of Britain, and one which has drawn much of its impulse from the Arabic and the African: the influence of Islamic religion on this writing has been markedly significant. Writing in

15 Adrian Roscoe, *Uhuru's Fire* (London: Cambridge University Press, 1977) 15.
16 Roscoe, *Uhuru* 14.
17 Roscoe, *Uhuru* 8.

Swahili is attributed to an African as early as the fourteenth century.[18] Indeed, there is debate as to whether Swahili or some form of Proto-Standard Swahili was being used on the east coast of Africa before the tenth century. Professor M. Guthrie in his article 'Some Developments in the Pre-History of the Bantu Languages'[19] records the percentage of 'general roots' in some two hundred Bantu languages, and he suggests that some form of Proto-Standard Swahili was being spoken on the coast before the tenth century (some centuries before the arrival of the Europeans). And although J. Knappert considers Swahili culture to be 'essentially oriental, not African in its material',[20] he is certain that the language of the oldest known preserved manuscript (1728) is so archaic that it (a Swahili text) cannot be dated later than the seventeenth century.[21] Whiteley sums up the feel of the eighteenth century when he records that the early poets 'seem to have lived and worked on the northern coast of Kenya ... writing religious and didactic verse in the Arabic script and using one of the northern dialects of Swahili'.[22]

The artistic, literary, and religious activity within Africa prior to the arrival of the Europeans was not merely confined to the one region of eastern Africa, as it is often suggested; for the Sudanic areas of west Africa had been active in Koranic scholarship for centuries, and literacy was achieved and being practised in the native west African languages of Fulani, Hausa, Mandingo, Kanuri and Songhai, though these have not received the amount of analysis given to Swahili.

18 Dathorne, *The Black Mind* 115.

19 M. Guthrie, 'Some Developments in the Prehistory of the Bantu Languages', *Journal of African History* 3, 2 (1962): 273–282.

20 Jan Knappert, *Traditional Swahili Poetry* (Leiden: E. J. Brill, 1967) 9.

21 Knappert, *Swahili Poetry* 3.

22 W. Whiteley, *Swahili, The Rise of a National Language* (London: Methuen, 1969) 18.

3. Oral Literature in West Africa

Unlike its written literature, unwritten literature in Africa has gone relatively unnoticed in the anthologies. But this point is true of oral and written literatures in other parts of the world, and therefore one need not make a special case for the west African situation. Still, the late twentieth century has seen some accounts that categorize oral literature as base and crude. The very popular assumption that writing is the basis for all other artistic expression has helped to create the belief that African literature is a very recent phenomenon. It is generally accepted that oral literature predates most forms of scribal expression; in Africa this is also the case.

Concomitant with and prior to much of the activity mentioned above there was in existence a tradition of oral art and literature. The evidence on the existence of African writing in periods predating British geopolitical involvement tells only half the story, since African life in itself is performative. This is a society built on ceremony, far from the early sketches of west Africans by 'emissaries of light', some of who painted a picture of apelike creatures with no form or comeliness and no culture. Still, a sizeable body of oral art, vibrant, ordered, and spontaneous, existed in many communities. This idea of absence of art would persist for years and continue up into the twentieth century, ignorant even of the nineteenth-century archaeology and its revelations about ancient Egyptian civilization and its sophisticated writing system.[23] But perhaps Dathorne comes close to the truth when, commenting on the role of the folk artist in some traditional African societies, he says of him that he is 'a difficult figure to understand, for his function corresponds to nothing comparable in present-day western society.

23 By 1822 the Frenchman François Champollion had deciphered Egyptian hieroglyphic writing.

He is at once inheritor and donor of the literature, its custodian and its liberator ... he has no personal voice'.[24] And T. Adeoye Lambo further explains how 'African traditional art was not as is the art of more contemporary societies, a luxury or a pastime.'[25] But the misreading of African culture had to do partly with cultural difference and partly with culturo-xenophobic posturing by a culture that had 'metre, rhyme (everything) that interests or soothes the feelings or arrests the passions'.[26]

A wealth of African oral literature has existed in poetry, prose, and drama, for a long time. Although Finnegan shows some reservation about the early enactments of 'drama' in Africa, where she suggests that the mid-nineteenth century might be one starting point,[27] one may still wonder about her assumptions as to what counts as 'drama'. If you begin with the Eurocentric notion, for example that linguistic content, 'specialized scenery', and 'the interaction of several characters'[28] must emanate from an enactment for it to be correctly titled 'drama', then a tradition which through its own evolution has placed much emphasis on dance, music, mimetics, and costume within performances might be seen to fall short of this label.[29] Perhaps Finnegan is not off the mark when (though for her own reasons) she opts for terms such as 'dramatic art', 'dramatic verse', and 'dramatic phenomena', staying clear of the contested word/phenomenon 'drama'. African drama has always been enacted within the market place or wherever communal activity has taken place, with no real need for what Finnegan calls 'specialized scenery'. Prose narratives, of which there are many in print today, are to some extent echoes of stories told

24 Dathorne, *The Black Mind* 3.

25 T. Adeoye Lambo, 'The Place of the Arts in The Emotional Life of the African', *A.M.S.A.C. Newsletter*. 17 January (1965): 4.

26 J. L. Döhne, *A Zulu-Kaffir Dictionary* (Capetown, 1857) ix.

27 Finnegan, *Oral Literature* 504.

28 Finnegan, *Oral Literature* 501.

29 Finnegan, *Oral Literature* 505.

orally throughout generations, and passed down to the present. It is easy to see how traditional societies can produce a wealth of narratives that possess notable form in terms of plot, theme, characterization, and delivery. In many ways there is a close association of these narratives with the field of drama, proverbs, oratory, and other forms of storytelling or address. They all facilitated the interaction of actor and audience, the two operating at the same level of understanding. Ultimately, the concern about what is and what isn't 'true drama' is perhaps best left to other studies whose central arguments depend on a protracted investigation of that issue.

The praise poet, the performer of religious poetry, the panegyrist, the elegiast, and the lyric poet had all been practising their craft before external forces sought to declare their practice obsolete. The European powers' restructuring of society in the realms of religious practice, economic activity, politics, and governance challenged the traditional artist. Most traditional poets belonged to all, and all belonged to them. They sang of 'kings and cattle':[30] such were the dynamics within traditional art in times when most Europeans had known little or nothing of Africa.

The state of the arts in west Africa should therefore be seen as having been affected by the European factor rather than initiated by it. The world of literature in Africa, more specifically western Africa, exists along a continuum of sorts. The role of Europe should be seen within this framework, for frequently there is a temptation to categorize west African literature as appearing in English and beginning to flourish by the mid-twentieth century.

30 Dathorne, *The Black Mind* 46.

4. A Perception of West Indian Literature: Continuity

The argument made so ardently for African literature (oral and written) as having predated the period of European (and more specifically, the British) influence, can also be raised in relation to West Indian literatures. Arguably, in the same way that 'preliterate' Africa was able to communicate orally and by use of its own scribal forms and representations, so too historians, anthropologists, and linguists can argue for the existence and practice of similar means of communication in the West Indies during the pre-European era. However, there is not that traceable body of indigenous written literature as can be found in much of western Africa. Whereas trade and encounters with east Africa led to the advance of west and east African writings, there has been no similar experience for the territories of the West Indies and least of all for Barbados, the most conservative of Caribbean islands. Furthermore, the practice of writing by Amerindians, specifically the Arawaks and Caribs, is not believed by the experts to have been at the level and relative volume of that produced among the Fulani, Hausa, and so on.[31]

But all of this is not to ignore those practices among the Amerindians which must count as elements of artistic expression: their various festivals and ceremonies connected with war, hunting, religious worship, and initiation rites. Ultimately, however, it must be said that writing gained some momentum with the introduction of formal colonial education.

There is substantial merit in the suggestion that the historical continuity between west Africa and the West Indies may indicate an African root for some West Indian literature. This is an underlying phenomenon. However, in many circles literature by West Indians is regarded as a self-contained category. It has its own space within journals and other kinds of scholarly

31 Geoffrey Parrinder, *African Mythology* (London: Paul Hamlyn, 1967) 12.

and intellectual writing. Although there are a group of writers who are deeply committed to maintaining the level of interaction between these two literatures, there are few contemporary critics who consistently treat both literatures under one heading. Even those former disciples of the Commonwealth literature ethos, are clear about the prevalence, persistence, and uniqueness of national literatures. In his essay 'Nationalism, Internationalism, Periodisation and Commonwealth Literature' Bruce King, who has produced much scholarly work of a general Commonwealth type, observes that 'the treatment of commonwealth writing as consisting of discrete national literatures will become increasingly common as the literatures evolve'.[32]

Sociologists, anthropologists, historians, and social psychologists all concede that the transfer of people from one setting to another results in changes which are far reaching; depending on the nature of the transfer, changes to lifestyle and personality may be minimal or drastic. The crossing was traumatic, even if cultural and other practices also made the trip. The anthropologist Melville Herskovits ('hervokitz' for Brathwaite in *X/Self*)[33] has highlighted the sense of trauma and discomfort experienced by the immigrants. The sociologist Fraser has also cited the psychological effects of this transmigration and a further dislocation imposed by the institutions of slavery: this frightful phenomenon resulted in some degree of alienation, and is what Walcott refers to in 'What the Twilight says: An Overture' when he says that 'Colonials, we began with this malarial enervation: that nothing could ever be built among these rotting shacks, barefooted backyards and moulting shingles'.[34] Ngugi notes that 'The African taken to the Americas

32 Bruce King, 'Nationalism, Internationalism, Periodisation and Commonwealth Literature', *History and Historiography of Commonwealth Literature*, ed. Dieter Riemenschneider (Tübingen: Gunter Narr, 1983) 10.

33 Edward Brathwaite, *X/Self* (Oxford: Oxford University Press, 1987) 85.

34 Derek Walcott, 'What the Twilight says: An Overture', *Dream on Monkey Mountain, and other plays* (New York: Farrar, Strauss & Giroux, 1970) 4.

and the Caribbean Islands thus saw his languages, names, dances, religions, literature systematically assaulted by the colonial plantation system'.[35] The assault on literature meant that something not necessarily new, but certainly transformed, had to be produced. This condition of exile and placelessness would haunt West Indian literature for a very long time.

5. The Rise of West Indian Poetry

In his *West Indian Poetry* Lloyd Brown lists the free Jamaican Black Francis Williams (1700–70) as having had 'the first known poem published by a black West Indian'.[36] However, one might question the extent to which Williams was indeed a forerunner of modern West Indian poetry: in many ways he was closer to the east African Latino than to anything else. For one thing, he wrote in Latin: also he showed a preference for panegyrics. His reading at Cambridge, where he studied, would have made him aware of Juan Latino's work, though few critics have made this point loudly; but it is safe to conclude that Williams's work was a conscious creation, a reflection of what he believed might develop into a style of writing that would be distinctly pan-African. Still, Williams's intention was not to be realized within West Indian literature, for although the panegyric is traceable within contemporary west African poetry it is not a conspicuous element within modern written poetryof the West Indies, whose subservience to Britain and its monarchs would have created a suitable climate for such a development (just as Latino had praised the Spanish Monarchy). This relative absence of the

35 Ngugi wa Thiong'o prefatory notes to *The Colonial Legacy in Caribbean Literature* by Amon Saba Saakana (London: Karnak House, 1987).

36 Lloyd Brown, *West Indian Poetry* (Boston: Twayne Publishers, 1978) 15.

panegyric in West Indian scribal literature might seem to buttress Long's opinion of the outcome of the Williams project[37] as being the exception rather than the rule.[38]

But the virtual non-existence of panegyrics in contemporary West Indian written poetry is not so much a matter of conscious choice as a result of the inequalities of racial and educational opportunity within the colonial era.[39] Williams had had access to a university education, a privilege which was not accorded the great majority of Black West Indians. The point should be made, though, that the panegyric is arguably more prevalent in West Indian oral literature.

Many years after Williams would come the Pastoralists of the nineteenth century such as M. J. Chapman and the Guyanese Egbert Martin, who was one of what Burnett calls 'The Guyanese narrative poets'.[40] He and his other contemporaries created what was one of the first West Indian national written literatures. One cannot overemphasize the impact that established European poets had on this epoch and on the development of modern West Indian poetry: but West Indian poetry of true distinction would only appear within the twentieth century. Both Marcus Garvey and Claude McKay, the former for his firm political beliefs, and the latter whose verse acquired a more universal register when he migrated to Harlem, were able to sound a chord of active protest within West Indian writing.

37 Williams was accorded an education in Europe as a test to establish whether Blacks could attain equal performance levels as Whites, given equal opportunity.

38 Long considered Williams's success an exception. But one should note that subsequent Blacks were not even accorded the facilities which were made available to Williams. See Long, *The History of Jamaica* 476.

39 In *The Black Mind*, 433–434, Dathorne accounts for the appearance of Africa in Caribbean literature as due to Haitian writing, through Guillén's Afro-Caribbean movement and through Europe's interest in 'primitivism'.

40 Paula Burnett, *Penguin Book of Caribbean Verse* (Harmondsworth: Penguin Books Limited, 1986) xlix.

The 1940s produced writers such as George Campbell, and it was here that an expansion of writing in English was witnessed unlike that of any previous decade. The expansion of West Indian literature benefited greatly from the founding of a number of literary magazines: *BIM* appeared in Barbados, *FOCUS* in Jamaica, and *Kyk-over-al* in Guyana, and these, along with some others, would be launchpads for later voices within West Indian literature.

Martin Carter emerged in the 1950s, and his voice of resistance echoed the tone and attitudes of earlier resistance poets such as McKay. Carter's verse reset the timbre within the Caribbean protest tradition. This decade also saw the migration of many West Indians to major cities, among them writers and poets looking for closer association with the publishing houses abroad. In the following decade the St Lucian Derek Walcott was coming into his own, and his autobiographical book of poetry *Another Life* (1973) was to distinguish him as a classic voice within West Indian poetry. All this does not ignore the sociopolitical realities of the twentieth century, when the Harlem Renaissance was a fillip for many voices such as McKay and Garvey. This Harlem phenomenon is widely regarded as creating the context for the internationalization of West Indian literature. The 1960s unrest, especially within the United States but also in Africa (Ghana and Nigeria), helped to sow the seed for a decade of experimentation and protest within West Indian literature. But the voices of protest from this period would be unlike those of earlier poets: these newer voices seemed less restricted by form. They therefore utilized the West Indian vernacular/idiom, the language of the folk, to present their verse to the nation, the region, and the world.

It is perhaps here in the 1960s that the worlds of the oral and literary traditions first met with any degree of mutual respect, interplay, and harmony. The ska beat was gaining much attention and on the verge of developing into its popular derivative reggae. Songs such as Marley's 'Dem Belly Full'[41] were lamenting the plight of the poor ('a pot a cook but de food nuh nough'), and Selvon's 'Calypso in London' and other selected writings were approximating the texture and effect of the calypso. Louise Bennett, who had been writing and performing for a long time before this, was only then becoming accepted. But the poet who would most noticeably appear within this period was the Barbadian Edward Brathwaite. His verse embodied the Black voice, and would add significant creative dimensions to the concept of vernacular poetry. This was the early evolution of 'Nation language'.[42]

6. The Artists

Edward Brathwaite (now widely known as Kamau Brathwaite) was born on 11 May 1930. He is a contemporary of writers like George Lamming, Derek Walcott, and Martin Carter, though these came into prominence before he did, since most of Brathwaite's popular writing dates from his thirties or even later. Brathwaite was born at a critical juncture in the evolution of Barbadian and Caribbean society. Just a few years after his birth were the riots resulting from the harsh economic and social conditions that remained from the slavery and post-emancipation period. As a result of these riots significant changes came about after the deliberations of the Moyne Commission. During the years of Brathwaite's childhood there was greater representation of the average citizen within government, and educational opportunities were made available to a

41 Burnett, *Caribbean Verse* 64.

42 Edward Brathwaite, *History of the Voice* (London: New Beacon Books, 1984) 13.

wider cross section of citizens, though not to all. Brathwaite was able to leave primary school and pursue a secondary education, partly due to his parents' better than average status, but also on account of his intellectual potential. During these critical years he spent memorable times at his uncle's dwelling at Mile and A Quarter in the parish of St Peter, in rural Barbados. There he encountered Pentecostalism and Shango. These events would return with nagging persistence within his poetry.

He did GCE Advanced Level examinations, and on gaining a Barbados Scholarship he left for Cambridge in 1950. After his time at Cambridge he arrived in Ghana after having applied for work in places as diverse as India, Israel, and Sri Lanka. His new homeland of eight years would etch the most permanent imprint on his sensibility and his art. He resided in a region that (along with Nigeria) was seen as the torchbearer of independence in the developing world. Brathwaite's experiences in west Africa would bind him to his homeland in some surprising ways. Two years after his return to the Caribbean the poetic collection *Rights of Passage* was taking shape: it grew out of an awareness of the fact that the journey across the Atlantic to the 'New World' centuries ago still held serious import for the people of the post-Independence Caribbean. Here was a man who had left his home, had traversed two continents, and would return to reveal his innermost perceptions: how he had changed, into what he had changed, and why.

Just as Brathwaite had been born into a society that was on the brink of great change, so too Okigbo's arrival at Ojote (a rural village) in the 1930s meant that he would be a product of the newly forged Nigerian society. Sunday Anozie nonchalantly proclaims that his family and Okigbo's were Roman Catholic.[43] This might suggest to his audience that Catholicism

43 Sunday Anozie, *Christopher Okigbo; Creative Rhetoric* (London: Evans Brothers Limited, 1972) 6.

had for centuries been dominant within Igboland and widespread; but an examination of the sociology of religion within Nigeria reveals that Christianity is a relatively new religion, and that traditional religion was practised long before, especially in the rural areas, where it has continued to dominate. This bifurcation of religious influence had a deep effect upon the lives of many Igbos of Okigbo's generation.

As with Brathwaite, there was no guarantee of Okigbo's acquiring anything more than a primary education. There were less than fifteen government schools in the region up to 1931.[44] Like Brathwaite, he benefited from his familial status; his father was a teacher at the time. But his acceptance into the one government secondary school within eastern Nigeria at that time also reflected his scholarly potential. He graduated from Ibadan University College, one of just eight hundred persons who were being received as undergraduates annually within the entire territory.

Okigbo was active during his time at university. He was involved in many extracurricular activities, including his favourite sport of cricket. He also had a fondness for music. His fondness for his nieces and his eagerness to write a book of children's verse reflected the impact of his formative years on his maturing sensibility.[45] Although he never came to realize this aspiration, his fourth canzona entitled 'Lament of the Lavender Mist' takes up the notion of childhood love, and (particularly) his 'Heavensgate' recreates characters from his childhood life: 'Kepkanly', 'Jadum', and so on. If the general perception is correct that the years immediately after his graduation were crucial to the maturing of his poetic talent, then he holds something else in common with Brathwaite.

In much the same way that Caribbean writers like George Lamming and V. S. Naipaul were setting the tone for West

44 Felix Ekechi, *Traditional Transformation in Eastern Nigeria* (Ohio: Kent State University Press, 1989) 98.

45 Anozie, *Creative Rhetoric* 6.

Indian literature, and calypsos were being sung abroad by such exponents as Lord Beginner and Lord Kitchener during Brathwaite's formative years, so too Okigbo's entry into the sphere of the arts was preceded by Africa's awakening interest in its own art. Wole Soyinka, J. P. Clark, Achebe, and Ekwensi were establishing themselves even before Independence, and painters such as Uche Okeke and Ben Enwonwu were making noteworthy contributions.

Quite unlike Brathwaite, though, Okigbo's work would take shape and culminate within a space of about ten years. His early death would lead to much debate as to whether he had reached his full potential as an artist, and as to whether his works were truly complete or if *Labyrinths* was but a partial revelation of a grander vision. Awoonor seems to suggest this in his play *Lament* by the reiteration of the phrase 'I was not ready' in response to Okigbo's death. In some ways Ali Mazrui's novel *The Trial of Christopher Okigbo* debates this issue of the artist versus the human being and the academic versus the activist. In it Mazrui has Okigbo defended by an unassuming protagonist. Throughout the trial there is debate on the duty of the artist to his art, to his nation, and to his self. Brathwaite's work has come under similar scrutiny. There are those who would consider his poetry as reflecting the tensions between private and public utterance.

These poets have in many instances explored similar issues, but they have also treated issues that are peculiar to their experience. Their methods are similar in some ways and different in others. The value of a study of this kind is that it opens up a discussion on two critically placed authors. Their work has hardly been given an adequate critical discussion that recognizes their contribution as near-contemporaries within two regions that drew support from each other. This study does not set out to trace the active influence of one writer on the other; rather, it demonstrates how the political, cultural, and spiritual climate of pre- and post-Independence Africa and the Caribbean shaped the sensibilities of the regions' leading creative artists. It examines their responses to the changes taking place around and within them.

Conclusion: Objectives, Scope

Above all, this chapter has sought to give greater perspective to the comparative analysis of the work of two poets. It has been necessary to examine and trace selected roots at the base of these literatures, especially within west African literature, whose oral and written traditions predated the European arrival by centuries.

All of this is aimed at giving this study the contextual background that it needs for a fuller appreciation of the artists under discussion and for a more profound comprehension of the critical comments to be made about both literatures. It has been necessary to mention the oral and folk traditions, since much of the poetry to be considered derives from within such a base. A salient point that has come out of this descriptive chapter is the intrusive nature of British culture into both worlds, and its impact on their literatures. What we have is a complex web of literatures and languages where British, West Indian, west African and a range of other features have interfaced for many years. The result is a traceable link in the 'third world' writings, especially in terms of theme (this is sometimes facetiously referred to as a political anachronism).[46] Walcott expresses what this web of experience means for the West Indian – indeed, for West Indian literature – in 'What the Twilight Says': 'something prickles in me when I see the word

46 Helen Tiffin makes this allusion in her article on 'Commonwealth Literature: Comparison and Judgement' in *History and Historiography* 19.

Ashanti as with the word Warwickshire, both separately intimating my grandfathers' roots both baptizing this ... hybrid'.[47] And Naipaul might make a similar comment in relation to his East Indian roots and his British conditioning; such is the diversity of influences within the literature called 'West Indian'.

So the implications for criticism and critical methodology are far-reaching, and the kind of work to be treated in this book should be undertaken with cognizance of the similarities and intricacies of distinction between West Indian and west African literature. This study is also a probe into the Black psyche, and it attempts to measure the workings of the intellect, soul, and will when impacted upon under trying conditions. Edward Kamau Brathwaite and Christopher Okigbo the men, therefore, also take on duo-macrocosmic symbolism as they come to stand for firstly their respective nations and their literature, and secondly serve as archetypes in the quest for personal and collective freedom.

Ultimately, what might evolve from an undertaking of this kind is the production of a work that enriches the field of comparative literature. T. S. Eliot's belief that there is 'an unconscious community' between the great writers of any time is (and isn't) borne out in the ambitious nature of this study, but Eliot's theorizing is in no way the raison d'être of this book; neither is Amanuddin's call for 'aggressive scholarship in commonwealth studies'.[48] This work does not attempt to offer the kind of close reading of the individual poets as a study devoted to a single author would do.[49] A more vital imperative here is to make critical connections between the works of these major

47 Walcott, 'What The Twilight Says' 10.

48 Syed Amanuddin, 'Towards A View of Commonwealth Poetic Tradition', *Awakened Conscience*, ed. C. D. Narasinghaiah (Kowloon: Heinemann, 1978) 423.

49 See, for instance, *The Dance of Death* by Dubem Okafor, which offers a close reading of Okigbo's private life and politics. (Trenton: Africa World Press, 1998).

poets from the two regions, artists whose work has scarcely been subjected to this kind of ongoing critical scrutiny. Hopefully, pioneering exercises of this kind can re-educate us about what we already know, as well as inspiring us to reach for new and exciting ideas and conclusions.

CHAPTER 2

Language, Culture, and the Artist

> Why shouldn't there be a Nigerian or West African English which we can use to express our own ideas, thinking and philosophy in our own way?[1]

> For the language in which these books are written is English – which, I must repeat – is a West Indian language; and in spite of the unfamiliarity of its rhythms, it remains accessible to the readers of English anywhere in the world.[2]

Few studies that conduct a comparative reading of artists from west Africa and the West Indies can do so successfully without considering the critical role that language and culture play in the fashioning of artistic works. The politics of language has certainly preoccupied many critics and academics throughout the 1980s and 1990s, especially as part of the drive towards theory. Postcolonial studies and postmodernist discourse brought renewed attention to the role of language in the struggle between competing cultures and competing systems of knowledge. Regional writers had long been aware of the central role of language in the anticolonial struggle. This chapter therefore concerns itself with culture and language. It recognizes that imperialism and colonialism are supported by a process of cultural re-engineering, and that language is often at the centre of this cultural process. This chapter does not set out to provide

1 Gabriel Okara, *African Writers on African Writing*, ed. G. D Killam (London: Heinemann Educational Books, 1973) 139.

2 George Lamming, 'The Peasant Roots of the West Indian Novel'. *Critics on Caribbean Literature*, ed. Edward Baugh (London: George Allen & Unwin, 1978) 25.

a comprehensive description of the critical function of language in the two regions under study; there are now many detailed descriptions and analyses of this kind for both regions. Rather, it endeavours to provide its readers with a clearer understanding of some of the more important debates and considerations about language, and its use, in light of the particular issues raised by these two major poets. It therefore makes the point that both writers were born into a society undergoing transformation. Nigeria's much bigger population and its two hundred and fifty languages made it a much more complex territory than the Caribbean in terms of communication and artistic display. Brathwaite's and Okigbo's indigenous languages and culture came under the potent influence of the colonial power. As these two writers produced their work they had to make sense of this cultural conflict and its repercussions. Their greatest task was to negotiate a pathway in the midst of this cultural tension. Either they could resort to a position that valorizes the indigenous language and what it represents, or they could embrace the colonizer's language, or they could attempt other kinds of strategic engagement and usage.

1. Tracking Language and Culture

In the epigraphs to this chapter both Lamming and Okara recognize the importance of language as a cultural marker. They are aware that language helps to define a people's identity. Language often assigns similarity or difference among a body of speakers. Like Okigbo and Brathwaite, these two writers are aware that the European contact with their region led to some erosion of indigenous practices, customs, and language. While colonialism depended on force and violence to bring about subjugation, it was through culture (and language) that colonial masters asserted their dominance and right to control. Lamming and Okara are convinced that their respective anticolonial movements need to enlist and employ their own regional and/or national language: but while Okara agitates for the establishment of a Nigerian form of West African, Lamming makes the suggestion that such a language already exists. He argues that the West Indian's use and performance of English is distinctive.

This similar yet divergent reading of the language situation in these early post-Independence societies reflects the kinds of paradoxes that arise in the work of many writers during the Independence period. The philosophical viewpoints about language, culture, and power are expressed in the actual experimental work of the various artists: so much so, that it might be suggested that the style of many writers of this period was driven by their very particular stance on the question of art, tradition, the Great Tradition, and the role and function of language in national development.

The two epigraphs by Okara and Lamming present a useful starting point for a discussion of which/what language is the most effective in the creative process at that and other junctures. But their statements cannot capture all the positions at work within this debate: there are too many. Within the Igbo context, for instance, there is someone like Obiajunwa Wali, whose novel *Ngozi Dili Chukwu,* written in bold and unabashed Igbo, is a testament to the sentiment that the vernacular is the most spontaneous and vibrant form, and hence is best suited as the vehicle for expressing African ideas. Positions like this challenge society to keep sight of its indigenous potential. Within this system of conceptualization the 'traditional' poet/artist is the voice of the people, and works for the people. Further, within this conceptualization modern West Indian and west African poets are often considered to be the descendants of the griot/crier/folk singer of the oral tradition, and like the Igbo village bard who leads the dancers with recitations at the yam festival, the modern poet is often being asked to assume a symbolic role at the forefront of national development. In *The Music of Africa* Nketia describes the oral poet and the audience's relationship to him:

> Those who came to watch and hear them may be familiar with their music, and may enjoy hearing what they already know, while listening to the creative variations that may be made in the course of the performance.[3]

Both performer and audience have quite common experiences and desires, which are mediated by a shared linguistic, musical, and mimetic enactment. The intrusion of another 'master' language and culture as a consequence of the colonial project brought about a set of changes. There were also socio-economic and political transformations that had far-reaching effects on conceptualizations of the artist's role.

In some African communities the shift of emphasis away from the oral mode of performance and towards the literary or written tradition had largely to do with the impact and demands of Euro-centric taste and attitudes upon the arts. Because of the prestige associated with writing (since it was initially the distinctive privilege of the masters), there began to be a distancing between the two modes of expression. Many new artists, including poets of the new emerging society, cultivated dreams of having their verse published in Europe, and being read by an already established literary audience somewhere abroad. Thus Dennis Osadebay, an Igbo and one of the 'pioneering' Nigerian poets in the English language, could sing the praises of his teachers in bright hymn-like metre:

> Thank you
> sons and daughters of Britannia,
> you gave me hospitals,

3 J. H. Nketia, *The Music of Africa* (London: Victor Gallancz, 1975) 32.

you gave me schools...
Thank you;...[4]

Some of his contemporaries in the West Indies felt no less indebted to the masters of this new literary project.

Limited educational opportunity and social inequality meant that the experiences which some of the new twentieth-century 'town criers' were espousing in print were not being captured by that audience which once would have known their verse and would have repeated it along with its performer. More traditional methods of communication gave way to other competing practices, and the role of the crier/poet took on a new dimension. Since an intended primary audience was European, Anglo-American literary artists were perforce the idols of many new poets. Eliot and Pound were some of those whose style was emulated, for they were the instigators of a changing attitude within Western verse.

The modernist movement had a significant impact on the language, style, and themes of many other writers of Okigbo's and Brathwaite's generation. Many of the ideologies and stylistic experiments that were central to the modernist project seemed in disharmony with the traditional formulaic folk methodologies of west African and West Indian artistic expression. For a starter, modernism stressed a greater sense of individualism, not only as a theme, but also as a stylistic marker of the artist. The modernist writer's prime duty was not to any group, society, or tradition, but rather to his/her work and the self-conscious celebration of art. The inculcation of this attitude was at variance with the more traditional and collectivist outlook of many West African and Caribbean societies (except for a few peoples, such as the Dahomeans and Yorubas).[5]

4 Dennis Osadebay, *Africa Sings* (Ilfracombe: Stockwell, 1952).

5 J. Cordwell, 'Continuity and Change in African Cultures', *Artist and Audience*, eds. Richard Priebe and Thomas Hale (Washington: Three Continents Press, 1979) 184.

By the time we reach the subjects of this book (whose major works emerge in the 1960s), it is no secret that the traditional role of the poet has changed. Dathorne makes this observation, but considers the transformation to have been a quite obvious process; hence for him the question is not so much 'for whom do they write' but rather 'on whose behalf do they write'.[6] For him it is not primarily a matter of language and style: theme and message are the critical components. Dathorne's observation seeks to uphold the view that there is a connection between the contemporary writer (say, of the 1950s and beyond) and his traditional counterpart by hinting at the persistence of the concept of the artist existing *for* the collective/community/ society.

Within the arenas of west African and West Indian literature there are ongoing debates about the way to be truest to one's tradition while not losing touch with a global artistic community. Quite often these two considerations are seen as oppositional, and language, or rather linguistic performance, is an indicator of the artist's affection and allegiance. Thus to the critic Peter Young a work like Obi Wali's *Ngozi,* which is in the vernacular, might be seen as 'a deliberate withdrawal into a linguistic and cultural privacy'.[7] In a sense his audience is chosen, due to the language variety he adopts; but why must it be seen as a withdrawal into privacy? Certainly Obi Wali feels no more restricted than does a writer who chooses the English language in preference to an even larger worldwide audience of Spanish speakers. R. B. LePage makes a similar observation to Young's, although his judgment appears a lot less biased, since

6 O. R. Dathorne, *The Black Mind* (Minneapolis: University of Minnesota Press, 1974) xiii.

7 Peter Young, 'Tradition, Language and the Reintegration of Identity in West African Literature in English', *Critical Evaluation of African Literature,* ed. Edgar Wright (London: Heinemann Educational Books, 1973) 25.

he balances the consequences of adopting an indigenous language variety against that of employing a global variety:

> If he uses the parochial dialect with which he is most familiar and perhaps most easily at home in a relaxed manner for telling stories or other intimate purposes he may find that he has only a parochial audience. Once he tries to aim at a slightly larger audience ... he enters upon a process of normalization.[8]

Given the pros and cons of this situation the poet – indeed, the writer – in west Africa and the West Indies is quite often attempting several types of compromises.

Egudu's and Nwoga's *Igbo Traditional Verse* is a translation into English of traditional Igbo verse, a process which has attempted 'to preserve, where it is possible, the original patterns of thought and imagery while not destroying the normal requirements of English expression'.[9] The formalizing of Igbo vernacular literature (in effect, its written form) is only a twentieth-century occurrence, which saw its first real practitioners (like Pita Nwana) coming to the fore at about the time of Okigbo's birth in the 1930s. Although a promising Central Igbo language emerged, the government machinery and the educated Igbo did relatively little to foster its adoption. In a discussion of the standardization of Igbo, Nwachukwu attributes the restricted use of Central Igbo not to the unpopularity of this dialect but:

> to the educated Igbo peoples' indifference to their language, and consequently to the values expressed in that language. For the educated Igbo pride and prestige are associated not with Igbo studies, but with

8 Robert Le Page, 'Dialect in West Indian Literature', *Critics on Caribbean Literature* 126.

9 R. Egudu and D. Nwoga, *Igbo Traditional Verse* (London: Heinemann, 1971) 5.

> things foreign and high-sounding, such as the classics, French, English, German.[10]

A great many writers, including Nwoga and Egudu, were therefore inclined to make fuller use of what had become their lingua franca, English; hence the process of communicating local, innate, natural 'patterns of thought and imagery' into a second language must have been a challenging one. Like Egudu and Nwoga, Achebe expresses a desire to confront the issues he treats, and says that he will use English; but he suggests a radical process of linguistic appropriation. He suggests that 'the English language will be able to carry the weight of my African experience. But it will have to be a new English still in full communion with its ancestral home but altered to suit its new African surroundings.'[11] His objective is not unlike that of some other great writers in other literatures (Irish, Indian). Achebe's method is bound up in a process of endeavouring to communicate the unfamiliar world of Nigeria to all who read his novels. Thus he becomes one of the better exponents of the craft of what Peter Young calls 'cushioning', which is all about teaching the reader without appearing to be too pedantic.[12] This he does through glossing of culture-specific words. While translating, he treats the Igbo proverb with care, and yet does not utterly confound the mind of the non-Igbo reader.

Okara has attempted a somewhat similar feat as Egudu and Nwoga in his *The Voice*, though in a unique way. He endeavours to approximate an African/Ijaw texture, cadence, and feel through a manipulation of the English lexicon, syntax, and morphology. His novella has not been spared its share of criticism, but certainly the reading of it provides a rewarding

10 P. A. Nwachukwu , *Towards an Igbo Literary Standard* (London: Kegan Paul, 1983) 14.

11 Chinua Achebe, 'English and the African Writer', *Transition* 18 (1965): 27–30.

12 Peter Young, *Critical Evaluation of African Literature* 39.

experience, one distinct from what you get in a conventional European novel:

> Okolo stood. They moved nearer and suddenly, pounced on Okolo. Okolo and the men fell to the ground. Hands clawed at him a thousand hands, the hands of the world. Okolo twisted, struggled and kicked with all his shadow, with all his life and, to his astonishment, he saw himself standing free. Out Okolo sprang and ran. The running feet came nearer, the caring nothing feet of the world. Okolo turned a corner and nearly ran into a boy and a girl standing with hands holding each other.[13]

Okara's penchant for the traditional Ijaw proverb, metaphor, and myth feeds his style with an element of naturalness, and the repetition of word items echoes 'the rhythms of traditional songs'.[14] The poetic qualities are indeed noticeable, quite close to what one might refer to as polyphonic prose.

Within the Caribbean area the absence of a standardized Caribbean English has given rise to various linguistic/stylistic approaches to literature. V. S. Reid has attempted modified linguistic varieties as he tries to capture the dynamics of a Caribbean speech continuum in *New Day*, while C. L. R. James presented a contrived dialect in *Minty Alley*, and Claude McKay became dedicated to the detached allusion (as is evident in 'Flame-Heart'). Among the poets Martin Carter, Dennis Scott, and the early Walcott seemed not totally persuaded about the multiple functions of their native language. Arguably it is with Roger Mais, Reid, and with Samuel Selvon's London and Trinidad short stories that a conscious, non-condescending effort to capture and transmit the feel of the West Indian language cadence is exhibited. Selvon's experiment is akin to Okara's in some ways: not so much in stated objective, but certainly in terms of effect, producing a fresh cadence, one

13 Gabriel Okara, *The Voice* (London: Heinemann Educational Books, 1964) 114.

14 Emmanuel Ngara, *Stylistic Criticism of the African Novel* (London: Heinemann, 1982) 39–57.

which goes beyond the conventions of the British literary models:

> The house get a kind of look about it, people afraid to even pass near it in the street. True a lot of the houses in London like that, but this one as if it threatening to collapse any minute. The landlady and she husband had was to move out and get furnished rooms, and the agent say he washing his hand of the matter, that it look as if the house have jinx, that nobody want to buy it.[15]

Descriptive passages like this one are interspersed with dialogues, sometimes between native speakers, and on occasion the vernacular takes over, as, for example, in a Louise Bennett poem, or as in this one by Bruce St John:

> De cashmere sweater dat yuh sen'muh so soft
> An so warm, uh kin nevah nevah furget muh
> Poor li'l chile. Sister Reed can'
> Brag pon me like before, tink she one got
> Daughter in England?[16]

Were Obi Wali writing as a West Indian he might produce a variety similar to St John's here. Like Obi Wali's work St John's and Bennett's oeuvres are considered to be folk material, primarily because these authors often write within the perimeters of national boundaries, employing the language of the masses and often presenting to the individual a candid image of his/her own lifestyle. Subject matter and style are thus often the chief criteria behind judgements of what is scholarly or popular verse.

Given the sociohistorical mindset which linked writing to erudition and scholarship and oral performance to base folk practices, there is still an inclination to categorize West Indian

15 Samuel Selvon, 'Obeah in the Grove', *Ways of Sunlight* (Washington: Three Continents Press, 1957) 174.

16 Bruce St John, 'Letter to England', *Caribbean Poetry Now*, ed. Stewart Brown (London: Hodder & Stoughton, 1984) 72.

and west African vernacular poets pejoratively as folk artists. However, this is not a foolproof system of labelling. It is not always that simple. In *Oral Literature in Africa* Ruth Finnegan makes a vital point about the specialized poet – the court poet – and his verse. She suggests that in the past 'the ruling monarchs and their ancestors were glorified in poems and real and ideal deeds were attributed to them in lofty and effusive language.'[17] This might serve to do away with the belief that there was one type of poet in traditional African society: there was not, and allusions to the poetry of the past always as 'folk based' might not be totally correct.

It should be recognized that performing in tandem with the griots and town criers of West Africa were panegyrists and other special-purpose poets. In many instances there was a distinction of roles among the traditional poets of Africa. Money and social status were also often important stimuli for poetic performers. The court poets and that body of independent poets who always sought close association with those in positions of authority (such as chiefs, priests, and royal figures) were to a great extent attracted by what Finnegan refers to as the 'greater luxury and leisure of court life'.[18] So what was oral was not always unmitigatedly folk: special-purpose poetry was demanded by certain occasions, and restricted to a certain audience not only on account of its closed setting but also due to its elaborate and sophisticated mode of expression. Contrary to some perceptions, oral poetry in western Africa could demand a great degree of specialized training, for there was in existence a highly formalized mode which demanded prescribed patterns of performance and delivery. But although some performances were restricted in terms of audience and 'high' style, the community/collective remained a valued group. It was the predominant audience; that group most called to be

17 Ruth Finnegan, *Oral Literature in Africa* (Nairobi: Oxford University Press, 1970) 83.

18 Ruth Finnegan, *Oral Literature* 86.

served, and it was to this group that the vast majority of oral practitioners turned for inspiration, patronage, and support.

Within the purely West Indian context, there were likewise certain performers who were called upon to serve specialized functions, just as in traditional African society. These might have been called to entertain the plantocracy at special parties and functions, or to act as private entertainers for their masters at various times of the day or night. But as obtained in their former country, these poets, now transplanted, continued to 'practise' their craft within the course of everyday activities whenever this was possible. There was no formal training, except for what was handed down from one practitioner to his successors.

In the West Indies the traditional folk singer/poet of West African descent came to realize the true worth of his/her talent when as a cultural or at times moral and spiritual leader he/she assumed a decisive tone of elevation or reflection, lament or ebullient revelry. In spite of the constraints put on much of their artistic performances, the early West Indian oral artists nurtured their talent well into the twentieth century as calypsonian, storyteller, reggae singer, and poet. These modern artists have achieved these titles because they hold one thing in common: their primary allegiance is to the masses, from whom their inspiration emanates, and for whom they invariably perform and write, whether directly or indirectly.

Christopher Okigbo came into West African verse in English at a time when it was undergoing its first phase of early development. Voices like J. P. Clark's, Soyinka's and his would prove to be the foundation, more or less, for modern West African poetry in English. With virtually no other 'formal'[19] indigenous models in Nigeria Okigbo, like the rest, was presented with the 'inevitable' option of turning to other sources. East African written poetry had developed much further than

19 'Formal' in the sense of being documented.

its west African co-tradition, and the concept of 'Negritude' certainly made east Africa a viable source of inspiration and influence. This potential remained unrealized, however, partly due to the colonial separation of the regions and to the language barrier between English and French – although there were those west Africans who did embrace the concept of 'Negritude' as an appropriate philosophy and response to their colonial experiences. 'Negritude' had been a term that became popular worldwide, but for Christopher Okigbo, and some others who received their university education at home or abroad in England, the attraction was to other more universally-acknowledged models. Classes on ancient Latin and Greek authors and attention to nineteenth-century British literature presented an attractive lens for viewing the literary arts, and reproducing their styles. It should be remembered that by this time there had already been creative artists who used traditional (oral) forms in creative writing, such as Wali and others; but these were in a minority, and regarded as outside the mainstream.

In a society where the growing debate was about how to be most true to one's national literature, Christopher Okigbo seemed not the least bit perturbed; he was more intent on exploring the workings of his soul, and on patterning his findings in his most elevated style: he was first and foremost a poet. This type of approach and many of his statements (for example, that he needed 'a more intelligent audience'[20] and that he believed he was 'writing for other poets')[21] have understandably exposed him to a great deal of criticism; and in an arena where one is labelled as either 'truly local' or 'universal',[22]

20 Louis Nkosi, 'Interview with Christopher Okigbo' in *Critical Perspectives on Christopher Okigbo*, ed. Donatus Ibe Nwoga (Washington: Three Continents Press, 1984) 242.

21 Nkosi, *Critical Perspectives* 239.

22 E. D. Jones, 'The Decolinization of African Literature', *Topaz* 21 (1968): 18–20.

it is not difficult to see where he was easily slotted. Chinweizu, Onwuchekwa Jemie, and Ihechukwu Madubuike have taken this a step further by revealing within Nigerian literature the clandestine presence of an academic faction. Okigbo's Latinisms and obscure allusions place him among this school of academics, referred to as the 'Ibadan Nsukka poets'.[23] The style of this clique is Euromodernist in orientation, and their work is regarded as inimical to traditional folk writing, which 'speaks a public language'.[24] They are in collusion with Eliot's Euro-based view of 'tradition'.[25] Chinweizu outlines the genesis and association of this clan:

> The Euro-modernist tendency was promoted into prominence in Nigeria during its years of emergence there (1957–67), and its best known practitioners in all Africa were Nigerians associated with the University of Ibadan and the University of Nigeria, Nsukka. These poets studied or taught at either institution and formed a clearly distinguishable literary coterie. They knew one another, cross-influenced one another, and were products of literary values and attitudes traceable to euromodernist teaching in these institutions.[26]

When Edward Brathwaite began to write, he too was faced with various possibilities and several challenges. As direct 'ancestors' he had the West Indian poets of the Romantic school, the landscape poets of the 1940s and 1950s, and the voices of protest in Garvey and McKay (rejuvenated in Roach and Carter). From abroad there was again Pound and Eliot (the latter's influence Brathwaite has acknowledged).[27] But at his

23 Chinweizu et al., *Towards the Decolonization of African Literature* (Washington, DC: Howard University Press, 1983) 165.

24 Chinweizu, *Decolonization* 188.

25 Eliot espoused a sense of tradition which was dependent on European models. 'Tradition and the Individual Talent' *Selected Essays* (London: Faber, 1951) 14.

26 Chinweizu, *Decolonization* 196.

27 Edward Brathwaite, *Contemporary Poets of the English Language* (London: St James Press, 1970) 129. But also, see Gordon Rohlehr's comprehensive

disposal as well were the potent strains of a submerged oral culture, which became more acute to him after his Ghana experience. The New Orleans experiment, jazz of Black America, and the co-existent counterforms of calypso and reggae (at that time ska) all became for him real alternatives as sources from which he could find material for the shaping of his craft. And he also saw his subject not too far away, in the everyday rituals of the folk. Brathwaite was not the first West Indian literary poet to realize and to utilize the unlimited resources that lay bound up in the actual practices of his indigenous society; nor was he the first to encounter the problems of attempting to fuse these popular folk forms into his work.

What Edgar Wright has said of African writers is equally true of their West Indian counterparts, for 'in practice' they were writers for a metropolitan market, primarily London.[28] This phenomenon has influenced the kind of writing produced by some authors. Some have romanticized the Caribbean, while others have appeared detached from the lifestyle they foreground. When C. L. R James undertook the novel (*Minty Alley*) about life in a lower-class yard there was a noticeable gulf between the writer and his subjects. The sense of detachment with which his authorial voice and the protagonist Haynes conduct their mission has become the West Indian critics' epitome of middle-class posturing towards the melodramatics of folk life. Practitioners of the West Indian pastoral poetic tradition were likewise accused of dabbling in local things because of a perceived glamour in the lifestyle of the folk. When Brathwaite's first major work appeared, therefore, there were many questions to be asked and many answers to be proffered.

work, *Pathfinder* (Tunapuna: Gordon Rohlehr, 1981) 3–20, for a perceptive discussion of Brathwaite's earliest published work between 1950 and1962 and its debt to – and subsequent emancipation from – Eliot.

28 Edgar Wright, 'African Literature: Problems of Criticism', *Journal of Commonwealth Literature*, 2, Dec. (1966): 108.

In a response to the first trilogy Ho Lung[29] spoke of Brathwaite's 'exotic' unreal world, Risden[30] contended that he 'offers no message to the heart' in *Masks* because of its public rather than private nature, and Walcott[31] caricatured Brathwaite as 'message-bearer for the millennium', 'celebrating the romantic darkness'. The demands on Okigbo were that he should draw more spontaneously on African (Igbo) resources, and that his work should be a lot less obscure so as to increase its accessibility to his fellow citizens. A principal criticism of Brathwaite has been his obsession with attempting to create sound and rhythm (supposed folk forms) at the expense (presumably) of sense: others have questioned his motives, asking whether his has been an interest only in folk ways, rather than in the folk themselves.

Brathwaite and Okigbo have found themselves under constant criticism. Some readers and critics have labelled their works as difficult. *Masks* is often regarded as 'hard', in spite of the glossary that appears at the conclusion of *The Arrivants*, and *X/Self* is an even more daunting collection. Brathwaite has also challenged a non-Barbadian audience to learn some of the peculiarities of his island, particularly in the two books *Mother Poem* and *Sun Poem*. This is not unlike what Okigbo has had to do as a means of making public his private world and also as a means of teaching his native audience. Attempting a compromise between nationalism and universalism, tradition and modernism, academic and folk concerns can mean that the poet's role is a dual one, at least. She/he must explain both 'Upandru' and 'Sam Lord', 'Urkella' and 'Sycorax'. So where the criteria for considering a writer and his work as academic or folk are con-

29 Richard Ho Lung, 'Sinner Fame Priest Raps on God and Culture', *Caribbean Contact*, 2, 9, December (1974): 19.

30 Winifred Risden, 'Review of Masks', *Caribbean Quarterly*, 14, 1&2, March–June (1968): 145.

31 Derek Walcott, 'What the Twilight says: An Overture', *Dream of Monkey Mountain* (New York: Farrar, Strauss & Giroux, 1970) 4,8.

sidered to be the incorporation of oral (folk) forms, the degree of privateness or publicness of voice, the loyalty to setting and theme (local v. universal), and the author's primary targeted audience (at home or abroad; folk or academic), it is evident that Okigbo and Brathwaite perform within both spheres. What one can undoubtedly say is that Okigbo's aesthetic doctrine as he entered the literary arena (as garnered from his interviews and writings) would put him into the band of writers who are more concerned with 'Art' than with the need to teach, although his later life and writing challenge this compartmentalization (symbolically, *The Trial of Christopher Okigbo* does not end with any definitive judgment). But were Okigbo to return to life in traditional African society he might be a court poet first, and folk poet afterwards.

Although ever since the late 1960s Brathwaite has been at the forefront of a movement which seeks to incorporate folk forms into the poetic establishment of West Indian literature, his work has none the less remained within the domain of academia. Is he the pioneer of a new movement in the Caribbean, or, as some critics have suggested, is he merely playing with sound (a superficial experiment)? Certainly, if popularity of one's work is a yardstick for measuring folk appeal in the same way that the 'road march' song defines the work embraced by the masses during annual Caribbean carnivals, then it must be confessed that Brathwaite is no more the people's artist than is the least-acknowledged calypso singer within his society. But perhaps we speak too soon and out of context, since the calypso is a popular art form and designed for mass appeal, whereas the 'literary poem' is not.

The debate is endless. But in conclusion, it must be said that Okigbo and Brathwaite are not easily labelled: there are dynamic forces at play, and it is too easy to assign fixed labels. A much more objective – indeed, rewarding (though difficult) – task is to explore the parameters of their stylistic and political endeavours.

CHAPTER 3

Creative Pathways in Selected Poetry by Kamau Brathwaite and Christopher Okigbo

In spite of the fact that some Caribbean and African writers share similar experiences of colonization, critical academic literature has not assimilated their various strands of interface and tension. This chapter considers aspects of the poetic work of Kamau Brathwaite and Christopher Okigbo. It calls attention to the ways in which they treat the concept/theme of creation, creativity, and creationism. The focus of this concept is not arbitrary, but provides an entry point for a better understanding of their response in the Independence era to the problems of history, colonization, art, politics, and personal and collective freedom. This exercise does not set out to be exhaustive; its primary focus is to continue to expand this area of fertile discursive possibility. It asks readers to contemplate the sometimes perceptible, sometimes complex web of relations that ensnares the creative process.

Okigbo's 'Heavensgate' begins with the initiate at the mercy of a greater power, or more precisely greater powers, since he is on the one hand requesting Mother Idoto's presence, and on the other seeks her protection against other forces: 'Dark waters of the beginning'.[1]

The Prelude to Brathwaite's 'Work Song and Blues', which is the opening section of *Rights of Passage*, resembles 'The Passage' segment of Okigbo's *Labyrinths*, in that the speaking voice is

1 Christopher Okigbo, *Labyrinths* (London: Heinemann Educational Books, 1971) 4.

heard making supplications to someone greater, against other forces:

So grant, God
that this house will stand
the four winds
the seasons' alterations
the exploitations of the worm.[2]

Another similarity that Brathwaite's poetry shares with Okigbo's is the recurring Biblical imagery. *Rights of Passage*'s 'you must mix spittle / with dirt' is a biblical allusion to Christ's mixing spittle with clay in an act of restoring sight to the blind. This act of restoration is confirmation of God's promise in moments of turmoil, as heard in Okigbo's psalmic overtones in 'The Passage':

... out of the depths my cry:
give ear and hearken ...[3]

Anozie offers the learned generalization that every poet 'begins like a prodigal' at the passage, quite similar to Okigbo, whose quandary is symbolized in the 'fire' and 'rain' imagery of 'Heavensgate'.[4] If 'New World A-Comin' from Brathwaite's *The Arrivants* can be taken as a parallel poem (if only because of its position at the virtual beginning of the text), then Anozie's generalization has some weight: for in 'New World A-Comin' there is a similar theme of loss of direction (leaderlessness) and spiritual vacillation, seen in the juxtaposition of 'O Lord' and 'O Devil'. Like Okigbo's persona, the speaking voice at the end of Brathwaite's 'Prelude' bewails his precarious standing with the metaphor:

2 Edward Brathwaite, *The Arrivants* (Oxford: Oxford University Press, 1973) 7.
3 Okigbo, *Labyrinths* 3.
4 Sunday Anozie, 'Okigbo's Heavensgate: A Study of Art as Ritual', *Critical Perspectives on Christopher Okigbo*, ed. Donatus Nwoga (Washington: Three Continents Press, 1984) 49.

Flame is our god, our last defense, our peril.

Flame burns the village down.[5]

Given these similarities, it might be tempting to invoke Anozie's reading as a universal truth about all poets and their poetry. This could lead to the dead-end summation 'so Okigbo has done this, but so have all poets.' This conclusion misses the mark, for there is the more fundamental issue of how – indeed, why – each of the two poets deals with the notion of exile and spiritual loss. The pleasure of comparing two poets like Okigbo and Brathwaite is that they share a number of similarities, but they are also different in some ways. This exercise is made even more worthwhile given the relative absence of extensive comparative criticism on the work of these major poets, who are both concerned with the artistic, political, and spiritual liberation of the individual and society in the post-Independence era.[6]

There is a virtual uniqueness about every poet's presentation and treatment of the spiritual quest, and this is true of as many poets as you can think of, even those considered to be as close as Pound and Eliot.[7] In much the same way that Eliot through such poems as *The Waste Land* and *The Hollow Men* was lamenting the stagnation of society and attempting an exploration of man's possibilities, Pound's *Cantos* was offering something new, giving a stir to this stagnation. There was a

5 Brathwaite, *The Arrivants* 8.

6 See one discussion of the two poets by A. R Yesufu, 'Ritual and the Quest for Selfhood in Okigbo's *Labyrinths* and Brathwaite's *Masks*', *NeoHelicon*, 28, 1 (2001): 236–245.

7 Walter Sutton, *Ezra Pound, A Collection of Critical Essays* (Englewood Cliffs: Prentice-Hall Inc., 1963) 3. In his introduction Sutton speaks of Eliot and Pound as 'fellow expatriates' and 'long time friends' among other things. Also see Elizabeth Drew, *T. S Eliot; The Design of His Poetry* (New York: Scribner's, 1949) 91. The author makes the point that Eliot and Pound collaborated in particular during the writing of *The Waste Land*.

measure of distinctness in each poet's vision of wholeness and wholesomeness, and in their poetic method. If Eliot saw hope for mankind through the bridging of the gulf set between man and God, then Pound was a humanist 'rather than religious and mystical'.[8] Sutton considers Pound's tradition, his method, to be 'eclectic'; he makes the point that Pound 'has drawn upon a great variety of past cultures for spokesmen and examples of the values he wishes to promote'.[9]

The initiate of 'Heavensgate' presents the first challenge to understanding Okigbo's spiritual experience. This initiate conceals as much as he reveals. He is a complex construct. The reader must speculate about his isolation. Over time his spiritual instability reveals itself as more than religious insecurity. The initial 'Easter sequence' of the early poems gives way to 'a process of sensuous anaesthesia' in the section called 'Distances'. Brathwaite also explores the spectrum of metaphysical experience, though not with such obsessive attention to one initiate. Brathwaite compiles the experiences of many dramatic personae while exploring the complexity of his own spiritual and existential experience: so in *Masks* the tribe stands for the poet, and in *Mother Poem* the female principle is as much female as it is male. To some extent it is Brathwaite's reliance on a multifaceted cast of archetypal characters (who appear and reappear) which endears his work to a broader and more varied audience. If the early Okigbo does not similarly convince a varied readership that the experience he is conveying is theirs as well, this is largely due to this poet's ultra-private voice.[10]

But in the final analysis the range of spiritual experiences that both writers explore, whether through a single persona or several, comes to represent the individual anxiety and collective consciousness of their nation. Herein is a great similarity between West Indian and west African verse of the Independence

8 Sutton, *Critical Essays* 7.

9 Sutton, *Critical Essays* 7.

10 Okigbo has stated that he believes his writing is esoteric.

era. The fragile yet fertile nature of the west African and Caribbean political systems becomes reflected through the work of their leading creative thinkers. Okigbo and Brathwaite are creations of their society. They therefore reflect the particular traits and anxieties of their culture. But they are also creators, in as much as their artistic work engages with the mythical evolvement of their nation, and projects a vision for future society; a vision that encapsulates the social, political, economic, artistic, and spiritual ambitions of the nation.

1. Creation, Creationism, Creativity, and the Quest

The notion of creation and creationism is more significant within modern west African and West Indian poetry than the body of published academic discourse on this subject would have one believe. Anozie's critical generalization cited above is in a way emblematic of the type of analysis that staves off further investigation. Too often this process of creation is simply a metaphor for the poet's artistic beginning and impetus: as Udoeyop[11] says of Okigbo, and as Rohlehr[12] says of Brathwaite's encounter in *Masks,* it is a signal that the initiation process has now begun. Concern often veers away from the act to focus on the actor and his actions. To highlight such a tendency in criticism is not to belittle the significance which the concepts of the beginning and of creation have within literature from the West Indies and west Africa but rather to point to the greater importance assigned to other conceptual issues.

11 Nyong Udoeyop, 'Okigbo: A Branch of Giant Fennel', *Critical Perspectives,* ed. Nwoga 55–56.

12 Gordon Rohlehr, *Pathfinder* (Tunapuna: Gordon Rohlehr, 1981) 116–118.

Creation and creationism have attracted much attention in the history of literature, and also over the centuries in other disciplines such as philosophy and mythology. Coming to grips with creationism can often be a first step to measuring the meaning of all subsequent acts of creativity. The creative writings of many authors of the European Romantic period (such as Blake and Shelley) make greater sense when placed within the context of their discourse on creationism and the artistic and spiritual quest. The literary critic cannot be chided for impinging on other disciplines if s/he through an analysis of creationism/creativity seeks to draw out an even more detailed picture of man's spiritual, political, and artistic destiny. This can be done by an understanding of how s/he comes into being, on whose account, and at whose expense. At whose expense, since belief systems such as Gnosticism have offered controversial ways of looking at the process of creation. For such theorizers God is not the all-knowing, all-loving, and all-giving figure he is portrayed to be in more conventionally accepted Judeo-Christian theology. In fact, He came to be seen as the arbitrator who proffered what was less than 'good'. The temptation of Adam was held to be the truly significant event. It was this way of looking at the world (where creator is creature, and the serpent is king), which became the model for some subsequent interpretations of life and the quest for life. Such enquiries sought to reconsider what was man's place in the universe.

The nineteenth-century revival of this ancient concept, now in Europe and under the guise of 'the Romantic creation myth'[13] again reflected an era's zeitgeist, revealing and dramatizing the anxieties of a time when it was not enough to draw inspiration from a Miltonic vision of creationism. In 'Stanzas in Memory of the Author of "Obermann"' Arnold alludes to 'the flood' of

13 Paul Cantor, *Creature and Creator* (Cambridge: Cambridge University Press, 1945) ix.

knowledge 'like waves on the beach', to sum up the attitude towards learning in that entire period.[14] The Rousseaus were busy dealing with concepts of man's original state and the state of nature. To some extent there was a 'pantheistic jumble' of spiritual beliefs.[15] All of this developed against the background of the burgeoning rise of science. So *Paradise Lost* gave way to *The Book of Urizen* by Blake, where his creator protagonist is a frightening power who reminds one of Milton's Satan; and then Shelley's *Prometheus Unbound*, where the apocalypse marks the beginning, and signifies the start of a process to know where man fits within the cosmos.

For the poet writing from an Igbo perspective, dealing with the concept of creationism and creativity is inevitable. Parrinder makes this clear when he comments on the vastness of west African religion, how it

> can roughly be depicted as a triangle. At the top, head of all powers, is God. On the two sides of the triangle are the next greatest powers, gods and ancestors. At the base are lower forces ... Man is in the middle and must live in harmony with all the powers that affect his life, family and work.[16]

West African myths of creation on a whole are as diverse as those to be found among other civilizations. Accounts of how life began are many and varied: from the Yoruban creation myth of Ol-orun the supreme being and creator, and his helpers the pigeon, the hen, and the chameleon (who spread the eternal dirt upon what is now called the earth), to the Kono (Sierra Leone) people's concept of how darkness came into existence through a bat's negligence in allowing his luggage of dust to

14 Matthew Arnold, 'Stanzas in Memory of the Author of "Obermann"', *Criticism and the Nineteenth Century*, ed. Geoffrey Tillotson (London: Athlone Press, 1951) 207.

15 William Courthope, *A History of English Poetry*, vol. 6 (New York: Macmillan, 1895) 78.

16 Geoffrey Parrinder, *African Mythology* (London: Paul Hamlyn, 1967) 15.

create night. But unlike the many philosophical and later literary movements that took root in other societies as a consequence of the pursuit of an alternative meaning to life by way of the redefinition of principles of creation/creativity, there was never among the Igbo that spiritual movement away from what was traditionally God's. The title of a Hausa proverb is pertinent: in it is expressed the immutability of the Supreme Being's unequivocal nature. The gods/spirits might be Janus-faced, but there is 'no king as God'; He is always good. For the Igbo traditionally there is the high god who is called 'Chukwu' to distinguish him from other minor gods. As creator his name changes to Chi-Okike; but these changes are linguistic transformations, and do not in any way point to mutability of being. As Uchendu notes, 'the idea of a creator of all things is focal to Igbo theology'.[17]

But what of modern Igbo society, what of societies influenced by the kinds of 'transgressive' thought to which Blake and Shelley were exposed? How is the artist able to make meaning of the creation of his life, of the spiritual significance of existence? How does the West Indian poet see his creation? Does it take place in Africa, in the West Indies, or elsewhere? Igbo and West Indian societies of the 1950s and 1960s were delicately poised as political and cultural systems. They came under the concentrated influence of both traditional and non-traditional forces. They were faced with questions of political independence, sovereignty, and the tensions associated with individual, collective, and national formation. The dialogics of this historical moment produced a creative impetus that artists seized upon. Artists themselves occupied a liminal space within society. They were themselves dealing with the complex question of their role in society, their level of participation in hot national issues, and their commitment to art itself. In effect, the

17 Victor Uchendu, *The Igbo of Southeast Nigeria* (Austin: Holt, Rinehart & Winston Inc., 1965) 94.

creation/birth of the post-Independence west African and West Indian artist paralleled the evolution of his/her society. The magnitude and depth of this complex matrix has found its fullest expression through the exploration of the spiritual and artistic quest.

2. Okigbo, Brathwaite: the Troubled Souls

The colonial encounter threw entire societies and civilizations into a cataclysmic gathering of wills. When Walcott visualizes the newly arrived slaves in a strange setting as trying to find their place in this repressive, 'uninhabited' landscape, he is confronting the same problem with which other poets such as Brathwaite are concerned. For Brathwaite the shipping of the African into the 'New World' has been so traumatic that the new landscape is without form and an unfriendly void; thus the need for ritualistic re-enactments of creation.

He is to some degree (though not totally) like the native citizen of colonial and post-colonial Nigeria, having to negotiate the competing systems of belief (mainly African and European). For the artist, one route towards fuller self- and soul-actualization is the re-examination of what the creative act consists of and what it produces. The problem brought on by the colonial encounter is a confrontation which persists: the pivotal battle is the struggle to reconcile one's position, either by reverting to one side of the dilemma (for the West Indian this means being faithful either to the ancestral land or the colonial power, and for Africans like Okigbo it means being obedient either to traditional duty or to modern 'progressive' thought), or by attempting a compromise of sorts. This attempt at compromise is not easily or readily achieved. Despite what has been written about both poets, it is the dialogics of hybridization that has most preoccupied them. Hence their protagonists and personae are often human beings in search of some measure of harmony, grounding, and fulfilment. They are troubled beings whose search within their souls is their prime route toward salvation and satisfaction. Thus the initiate of 'Heavensgate' and such characters as Brother Man in *Rights of Passage* are archetypes of troubled personalities. They are well aware of the politics of compromise, and respond to them in various ways.

3. Okigbo. 'Naked I stand': Initiate/Activist/Priest

The downpour of water imagery in the early sections of *Labyrinths* calls to mind some of the west African creation myths that take place in an overabundance of water. There is the Yoruban myth of Ol-orun[18] (who had to cover the watery earth with land), and the Fon story of the sea-dwelling children of the creator Mawu.[19] The first section in 'Heavensgate', 'The Passage', gives an indication that Okigbo is to concern himself with the idea of creation/creativity, and he intimates that coming face to face with this phenomenon helps to define the pathway towards understanding the meaning of the self, and sculpting one's identity. From early on the protagonist is found amidst

> Dark waters of the beginning.
>
> Rays, violet and short, piercing the gloom,
> Foreshadow the fire that is dreamed of.[20]

18 Geoffrey Parrinder, *African Mythology* 20.
19 Parrinder, *African Mythology* 21.
20 Okigbo, *Labyrinths* 4.

The storm imagery that accompanies the nebulous ushering forth of life (light) is a flashback to the presence of this atmosphere in many African creation myths. The serpent image is also an integral component. In 'The Passage' it is 'the boa'. The Ashanti tell of the python which is responsible for man's sexual awakening,[21] and this symbolism is also imbedded within some Western Christian accounts.

The 'Dark Waters of the Beginning' metaphor is commented on by the likes of Anozie, Udoeyop, and Udechukwu. Anozie rightly suggests that this genesis sequence might refer to either 'a mythical projection of a personal experience', or the recreation of 'the process of creative intuition';[22] Udechukwu narrows it to Okigbo's childhood experience. There is significant merit in all these positions. Udechukwu's insight is particularly relevant here, although he goes no further in specifying and analysing these claims. But in light of this interpretation it is useful to take cognizance of the sociocultural practice among the Igbo, where children are practically born into the world of adults.[23] There is no private world of children as is the case with other societies, and it is probable that this type of experience might have left (at least) a subconscious impression on Okigbo's psyche, one which could later serve as a social indicator as well as a metaphor for his spiritual initiation.

For some readers, Mother Idoto is merely one of the many Igbo gods. But besides being the river god (Anozie), and the muse to whom the poet confesses his nature (Udoeyop), she is also associated with the creative process: and the totems for her worship (among which is the python) must bring much validity to this claim that she is at the heart of the poem's discourse on creation. The extent to which Okigbo was consciously infusing her with traits similar to the Igbo earth goddess Ala (whose

21 Parrinder, *African Mythology* 50.

22 Sunday Anozie, 'Heavensgate', *Critical Perspectives*, ed. Nwoga 48.

23 Victor Uchendu, *The Igbo of Southeast Nigeria* 61.

status at the centre of the Igbo pantheon of gods has been heavily debated), cannot be defined with certainty; but there are some marked similarities. For one thing, Ala is also the god of fertility and productivity. Perhaps Okigbo is one who has subscribed to a certain Igbo view that the female principle is at the centre of human creation. In this case she can be seen in 'The Passage' as the all-powerful, all-good creator who stands apart from her Igbo worshipper, and who must always be approached in earnestness and with candour. Then it is she who has given life to the likes of the initiate (though he is not sure of this), and his encounter with her is a prelude to achieving fuller self- (and 'other-') awareness.

It is not totally clear who/what actually creates the world in Okigbo's *Labyrinths,* but you know that the process has not been easy, given the proximity of the paradoxical symbol of the 'boa-like rainbow bent to kill'. The tendency among many critics is to see this paradox (continued in 'rain' and 'sun', 'fire' and 'rain', 'wagtail' and 'sunbird') as no more than a metaphor for the conflict between traditional and Christian forces within the initiate's world. For Udoeyop the question seems to be 'who is the real saviour?' But the effort of salvation is the final step in ritual; hence it cannot be with this that the initiate now grapples. He is within these earlier sections concerned with 'who is the real creator?'.[24]

In the end the initiate makes us feel that he is sure of very few things, and that he does not know who is his creator. He is sure that his world begins with chaos and with 'combat', and this seems – at least at first glance – to echo the nineteenth-century European Romantic creation outlook. But whereas in those myths it was the creator who was at times also incomplete and at fault, in 'Heavensgate' there is no doubt that the initiate is the one at fault. It is possible to see Mother Idoto as a kind of Imo Miri, a spirit of the river before whom people

24 Nyong Udoeyop, 'Branch of Giant Fennel' 57.

swear their innocence: those who swear falsely are liable to drown in the same river or 'to suffer from waterlogging disease'.[25] Such might be the case with Okigbo's initiate. He has no quarrel with the creator, but sees himself as the one who cannot properly interpret the process of creation that has taken place. So he must undertake this quest, in some respects similar to that of Tutuola's palm-wine drinkard, and it is only at the end of this process that self- and 'other-' recognition is possible.

As Okigbo's initiate falters in the early stages of his birth, the reader observes the poetic juxtaposition of personal and grand mythical references. The numerous allusions to specific personages within Okigbo's private world of tutelage demand footnoted references for clearer grasp of the poem. The employment of traditional Nigerian and Western mythical figures also demands some editorial intervention. Okigbo's work therefore appears to sit tensely on the fulcrum of a well-wrought strategy. The reader cannot ignore the dialogue that the poet is setting up between a set of binary opposites. He asks the reader to behold the tension between the private and the public, colonizer and colonized, self and other, individual and nation, and between religion and extra-religious experience. Okigbo's *Labyrinths* does not reconcile all these opposites. The poet wants the reader to work them through, though he gives greater relief to some of these situations than to others. In particular, the *Labyrinths* collection works at reconciling the spiritual and political dichotomy. As the collection develops one gets a clearer understanding of how the spiritual deficiencies of the earlier sections are directly proportionate to the lack of political commitment on the part of the initiate. So that when in the latter stages of the collection, 'Path of Thunder', its poetic tone is strident, assured, and exultant, the persona is not only political activist, but also spiritual seer and town crier. The poems of this final section are political utterances, but they are also ritualistic

25 Victor Uchendu, *The Igbo of Southeast Nigeria* 98.

incantations. The town crier therefore returns as artist, political activist, and priest.

4. Myth-Making

Section 21 of 'Noom', *Sun Poem,* reveals a kind of beginning, a creation if you will; the process which has given birth to the Islands 'when the loa came out of the sea'.[26] This initial act takes effect at a Caribbean location (the east coast of Barbados), geographically closest to the world of myths and beliefs from which Okigbo has drawn most heavily in describing his creation. It is no surprise that this process is tempestuous as well, like the 'Dark waters of the beginning' in 'Heavensgate'. That the 'loa', the divine power of Haitian vodun (itself a derivational term of definite west-African origin) should be creator here seems to make this world at least partially dependent on the principles that helped to fashion traditional west African mythology. Brathwaite had previously dealt in greater depth with these principles in the earlier African sequence *Masks*. The difference between these two instances, however (creation in *Masks* and in *Sun Poem*), is that the one has its setting in Africa and the other is more properly situated in the West Indies, and seems more intent on tracing a West Indian mytho-philosophical poetics. If this is indeed the case, then *Sun Poem* seems to pronounce that the 'New World' creation process is neither an all-New World, nor all-Old World process.

'Legba', an Afro-West Indian god, is the name given to the loa, the creator in this section of Brathwaite's work: the process is awesome and has relied on several factors, but is successful. This version of the creative moment is also a critical response to

26 Edward Brathwaite, *Sun Poem* (Oxford: Oxford University Press, 1982) 51.

arguments that profess Adamic beginnings for West Indian man and those which suggest that nothing has been created in the West Indies.

The process of creation can never be straightforward. As observed in Okigbo's work, the fact of creation seems to throw into being its opposite: destruction. Brathwaite has given much attention to the interplay between the destructive and the creative in the fashioning of Caribbean society. For instance, in the poem 'Wings of A Dove', one of the more spirited, committed pieces in all of *The Arrivants*, the rhythm and language of the protagonist Brother Man echoes Elijah's evocations on Carmel; but whilst Brother Man is vociferous about the destruction of 'Babylon's boom town' he has no viable alternative, save only his utopian 'back back to Africa'. Through this New World archetype Brathwaite undermines the expectation that Africa holds all the answers to the creative destiny of the Caribbean. In his poem the destructive pales in the presence of the creative, and the new product appears a more worthwhile thing than that which it was/is not.

The chaos associated with creationism in 'Noom' is a controlled one. It is not a homage to the philosophy of Gnosticism, propagated during the Romantic creation-myth era. For one thing, the creator of *Sun Poem* is the central actor of 'Noom', and the reverent repetition of 'how' in the early segment makes it clear that the loa is supreme, though not aloof:

> how he must have felt when he reached the / shore ... how he must have paused in that sky-blue air ... how he must have made huge prints in the sand ...[27]

His presentation wins our admiration, since he can appreciate the tragic human emotions and conditions of pain:

> the sea-wind cold on his belly giving him plimper

27 Brathwaite, *Sun Poem* 51.

and ambivalence:

> once he had stopped turned looked back at his home

and a type of death:

> and his cry grew greater as the pain of the world grew black for
> him and he stopped and fell slipped staggered and fell down
> hackletons cliff down past the few bent coconut trees ...
>
> *'he dead where you stannin now' said the cattlewash boys.*[28]

All in all, a certain reverence and awe is invoked as the loa's expansive handiwork comes to mirror the widening of experience of the protagonist/son. The eastern/Atlantic side of the island in the poem symbolizes another side of life: the rugged, the untamed, the unknown, and the unconquered. For the initiate (whose name is symbolic), the process of creation is a gradual unfurling of life in its physical, social, and psychological aspects, as a description of the son Adam highlights:

> when adam walked out on the long redwood pier of his thoughts
> he found a new world opening out inside ...
>
> for growing up was finding for the first time there was other sea
> behind the high hills of the island's other shore.[29]

For Brathwaite the symmetry of experience for both creator and creature (where each, God and man, moves around in this milieu with a sense of reflective dignity and willingness to navigate and negotiate), is a consequence of the divine encounter. This results in experiential and epistemological adjustments for all manner of arrivants, all peoples and beings who act out their desires in the new landscape (Brathwaite would later explore these adjustments in works like *X/Self* and *Born to Slow Horses*). Here the poet would seem to intimate that the master and the

28 Brathwaite, *Sun Poem* 52.
29 Brathwaite, *Sun Poem* 39.

slave are both displaced in the colonial enterprise. For if the divine creator stands in awe of the newly created space, what then of lowly human subjects?

Brathwaite's compression of political and historical events within a mythological discourse seeks to call attention to the cosmic magnitude of the collective experience of Caribbean subjects, but also the innate passion of the artist in a new emerging nation. Brathwaite's creative myth-making seen in *Sun Poem* had previously been explored in *Rights of Passage* in the poem 'Calypso'. In his public lecture *The Artist and his role in Barbadian Society* given in Barbados during 1987 Brathwaite was clear on the meaning of the boyhood practice of 'skidding' a rock across a pool of water to see it submerge and emerge several times. It represented the emergence, baptism, and re-emergence of the creative spirit, and also the emergence of the Caribbean islands from the depths of the ocean.

> The stone had skidded arc'd and bloomed into islands:
> Cuba and San Domingo
> Jamaica and Puerto Rico
> Grenada Guadeloupe Bonaire
>
> curved stone hissed into reef
> wave teeth fanged into clay
> white splash flashed into spray
> Bathsheba Montego Bay[30]

The location called 'Bathsheba' in the poem is on the east coast of the Barbados. It is also the site of the creation in *Sun Poem,* and its association with other pan-Caribbean towns and/or islands from Cuba to Bonaire is a signifier of the spatial reference with which Brathwaite has been working from as early as *Rights of Passage.* Brathwaite's philosophizing in *Sun Poem* therefore has a national and pan-Caribbean dimension. The second section of 'Calypso' in *Rights Of Passage* uses the

30 Brathwaite, *The Arrivants* 48.

symbolism of creation to help explore the sociohistorical, political, and economic origins of contemporary dislocation:

> The islands roared into green plantations
> ruled by silver sugar cane
> sweat and profit
> cutlass profit
> islands ruled by sugar cane.[31]

So too, section 22 of 'Noom' in *Sun Poem* explores the beginnings of sociopolitical, economic, and cultural exploitation in a world opened up to those who were forced to cross the 'dark and dangerous outline on the silver line of the horizon':[32]

> Soon after the blacks arrived plantations prospered
> rivers of green flowered through valleys and up into the hills
>
> white stone houses with green roof tops appeared
> windmills retaining walls aqueducts
>
> the slaves built themselves boxes of limestone
> with black wooden shutters.[33]

The poem goes on to explore the Caribbean creation myth. In the final analysis *Sun Poem,* like *Rights of Passage,* is about the birth of the poetic and spiritual sensibility. Creationism in Brathwaite's early work therefore functions to focus and refract a latent, though pervasive artistic, philosophical, political, and spiritual preoccupation of this Caribbean visionary.

The work of these two poets reveals a concern with the various possibilities that pervaded their society when they wrote in the Independence and early post-Independence era. Although these poets did not rely solely on the religious/spiritual metaphor to open up their discursive treatment of historical, social, and political issues, it is evident that they both

31 Brathwaite, *The Arrivants* 48.
32 Brathwaite, *Sun Poem* 52.
33 Brathwaite, *Sun Poem* 53.

revered the potential therein. Where is an individual and nation's soul better contained, than in their religion? Creation, birthing, initiation, baptism, salvation, death, and rebirth are all common to the pursuits of religion and of life. If Okigbo's smaller collection of poems allows one to observe the work's movement from spiritual and personal endeavour to ritualistic and public enterprise, Brathwaite's oeuvre is much more complex to summarize (given the fact too that he is still adding to it). It is, however, possible to conclude that somewhat like Okigbo's, his poetry navigates the interplay between spiritual and social realms of experience. Like Okigbo, here is a poet who wrestles with the various tensions at work within the society and within the soul, and who places his life's work on the altar of human enlightenment.

CHAPTER 4

The Okigbo Music: A Study of 'Distances'

The artist's expedition into the realm of religious and spiritual ritual should hold some significance beyond the act of re-presenting an experience for its own sake. Okigbo's claim of not being sure about the meaning that much of his work conveys beyond the fact of the experience is nothing new in the domain of the arts, and of literature in particular. Many writers have from time to time claimed to be oblivious of the 'truth' within their work: Baudelaire readily comes to mind. The Spanish poet Federico García Lorca has claimed that he writes under the total inspiration of a 'dark/black' muse 'Duende'. Lorca's influence on Okigbo and their relatedness is merely alluded to within criticism on Okigbo, though they share more similarities than are generally acknowledged.[1] Later in this chapter I will highlight some of these similarities as a way of better interpreting the purpose (hidden or otherwise) of Okigbo's continuing quest within 'Distances'. But this chapter is less about Okigbo and the influence of Lorca, and more about exploring the meaning of Okigbo's quest within the collection 'Distances'.

It should be stated that whereas 'Heavensgate' and 'Limits' are predominantly about the spiritual experience of a tentative entrant, 'Distances' presents the maturing philosophy and style

1 In his introduction to *Labyrinths* (London: Heinemann Educational Books, 1971). Okigbo makes a fleeting reference to Lorca's influence In his essay on 'Fantasy or Dialectic' Anozie briefly refers to Okigbo's and Lorca's similarity as being based on the notion of possession. See also, Sunday Anozie's 'Distances: Fantasy or Dialectic', *Critical Perspectives on Christopher Okigbo*, ed. Donatus Nwoga (Washington: Three Continents Press, 1984) 32.

of an individual mind in its metaphysical workings under the influence of a medically-prescribed drug. Anaesthesia is however not the central thing here: it is merely a 'physical' facilitator which on one occasion gave birth to a type of spiritual experience quite like that achieved through a religious ceremony. The experience of 'Distances' is an extension of that explored earlier in 'Heavensgate', in that many of the motifs are still present. This is also true of Brathwaite's early poetry, even reaching back to his work of the early 1950s. If Brathwaite's first collection *The Arrivants* holds one thing in common with Okigbo's seminal collection *Labyrinths,* it is that they are both constructed around well-stated motifs: musical motifs are especially present. But perhaps unlike Brathwaite's first seminal collection, Okigbo's *Labyrinths* was not deliberately constructed to sound as a tightly woven composition. There are some moments of tension within the work's structure, but these are also moments of creative difference. 'Distances' is like the other sections mentioned, but it is also different in some respects. Ultimately, the major concern of 'Distances' shifts away from a thematic concern with religious, sociohistorical, and cultural problems and focuses on the process of artistic influence. 'Distances' is less directly religious and less spontaneous from its inception.

In 'Heavensgate' and 'Limits' one's attention is almost always focused on the muse. We find a similar fascination with higher creative power in the work of Kamau Brathwaite. His sea loa in *Sun Poem* introduces his poem's insistence on the higher creative power as critical to self-empowerment. Okigbo assumes the same focus throughout the early sections of *Labyrinths,* in order to define God and man as the principal actors within his discourse, thereby calling attention to this thematic imperative. Whereas the external force is the prime source of inspiration and power in the foregoing sections, 'Distances' is much more introspective – a journey into the self, a process predicated in 'Heavensgate' but not significantly and meaningfully undertaken until 'Distances'. I am almost tempted to suggest that Brathwaite's *Masks* – the second collection within *The Arrivants* – reveals a parallel process where the poet goes to the root cause of the source of exile, examining the African's (Omowale's) psychology and inner soul. I discuss this process more carefully in a subsequent chapter.

In his essay 'Okigbo's "Distances": A Retreat from Christ to Idoto', R. N. Egudu shows reservations about prominent critical approaches which tend to emphasize 'not a spiritual but an artistic quest in "Distances"'. He himself seems to prefer to see it the other way, that is, to see 'Heavensgate' and 'Limits' as an artistic quest and 'Distances' as a spiritual one. There can be much danger in attempting to categorize these texts in this manner: it might require a perspective which is privy to much more information than Okigbo has communicated to us, and much more than now remains, to prescribe the 'true' interpretation of his quest(s) throughout *Labyrinths*. One can be sure that it is equally possible to associate either the spiritual or artistic quest to the 'separate' undertakings, or one to both, or both to each. The critic might feel it his duty either to uphold the more literal approach that sees it all as the common religious rite, or one might see the religious ritual as a metaphor. In any case some credit should be given the poet for creating these insatiable possibilities.

When Okigbo revealed that his 'Heavensgate' was a contribution to his oft-neglected responsibilities of 'carrying on the various periodic rites which were connected with the worship of Idoto',[2] this was the closest we may come to starting a tentative labelling of his quests. *Labyrinths* is one sustained poem, and the spiritual quest runs through the entire work. However, the spiritual/religious undertaking of 'Heavensgate' and 'Limits' soon gives way to another concern with the inner

2 Okigbo in his interview with Robert Serumaga, at the Commonwealth Arts Festival, July 1965.

workings of the individual's soul, and with the process of communicating these innate developments.

For Lorca, the encounter with his muse 'Duende' could not be totally rewarding unless that experience could show some overt effect within his writing (and it does). Much of the insight that his work revealed (e.g. *El Romancero Gitano*), especially with regard to his symbolic portrayal of victimized gypsies, was due to the inspiration of his muse. So the muse appears only as a catalyst, the means to an end. In a similar way Okigbo's experience under general anaesthesia is a catalyst to his larger concern of defining and coming to grips with his newfound spirituality. This manifests itself through a more conscious preoccupation with form in 'Distances'. What is distinctly unique about this segment is its ever-audible strains of music: a music that accompanies this most unique of inductions. So now the onus is on the reader to make full sense of these melodies of which we generally know little, but which are the only guide to gauging the effects of this artistic undertaking. Okigbo's music is one of inward voices:

> From flesh into phantom on the horizontal stone
> I was the sole witness to my homecoming …
>
> For in the inflorescence of the white
> chamber, a voice, from very far away,
> chanted, and the chamber descanted, the birthday of earth,
> paddled me home through some dark
> labyrinth, from laughter to the dream. (53)

These inner voices are contrasted with an outer silence, of which Okigbo seeks to make sense:

> But what does my divine rejoicing hold?
> A bowl of incense, a nest of fireflies? (53)

Can he (how can he?) outwardly verbalize these inner melodies? What language, indeed what kind of language, can he employ to communicate the truths of his experience, so that it maintains some measure of sense, reality, and relevance? In an essay on '"Distances": Fantasy or Dialectic', Anozie is not prepared to monitor the extent of the 'metaphysical fantasies' within Okigbo's work, since he believes 'that if it is worth anything as art at all any poem ought to have it in itself to disclose and also communicate using its own authentic system of linguistic symbols ... A poem is not a metaphysical fantasy. It is a form of human communication' (132–133). One senses that Anozie is firstly speaking at the conventional level of the written word on the page. He decries poems like Okigbo's 'Distances' which seek to vicariously communicate the sentiments of a metaphysical experience. Yet in his approach to the symbolic word in Okigbo's 'Distances' Anozie's method tends to further complicate an already abstruse poem. He offers the formula:

P = D1+D2 a=D3+D4+D5 r = D6 (146)

The riddle of Okigbo's music cannot achieve its fuller interpretation through this 'scientific' analysis and expression. As the ongoing spiritual experience grows increasingly introspective, it takes him further into a world that places little confidence in the word. The signifier and the signified become disparate entities. In 'Distances' the word becomes replaced by sound (and the song) as the most significant and functional symbol of communication. Thus, from a critical perspective theme is replaced by form, technique, the allusion, and symbolism as the prime source of concern in the work. This is what Okigbo was alluding to when he spoke of it being possible to communicate meaning other than through the intellect. Like Brathwaite, Okigbo understood the challenges presented by the page. He contemplated the limitations but felt it imperative to attempt the notation, to give voice to the noise and disquiet that reverberated within his consciousness.

The entire section 'Distances' resounds with conflicting melodies. For example, there is the intrusive unnerving laughter which breaks the introspective mood of ('Distances I'), whilst ('Distances V') is a symphony of interchanges between the 'effervescent' utterance and 'silence'. The result of such arrangements is to create verse whose mood borders on crazed hysteria. The poet works and reworks this compositional structure of verse (with notes and rests)[3] and this technique evolves to re-emphasize emotional incoherence as an accompaniment to the spiritual/artistic process. In ('Distances V') the initiate has not yet fully understood the work that is going on within his soul ('the question in the inkwell'); nor can he control the movement of conflicting forces about him. So the fifth movement must reflect a type of emotional antagonism, and contradiction through its laughter/silence song play:

> each step is the step of the mule in the abyss –
> the archway the oval the panel oblong
> to that sanctuary of the earth's molten bowel
> for the music woven into the funerary rose
> the water in the tunnel its effervescent laughter
> the open laughter of the grape or vine
> the question in the inkwell the answer on the monocle
> the unanswerable question in the tabernacle's silence – (58)

In *West African Poetry* Fraser seems foremost to hear 'a song of hope and rejoicing' in 'Distances'.[4] But far from that optimism, Okigbo has heightened the nexus of emotional insecurity through a more direct method of juxtaposing antithetical conditions and states: from 'Flesh into Phantom' in ('Distances I'), to the assemblage of contrasting forms/shapes in ('Distances IV'):

> And at the archway
> a triangular lintel
> of solid alabaster

3 Léopold Senghor deals with this phenomenon in *La Parole Chez Paul Claudel et Chez les Négro Africains* (Dakar: Nouvelles Editions Africaines. 1973) 50–51.

4 Robert Fraser, *West African Poetry* (Cambridge: Cambridge University Press, 1986) 127.

enclosed in a square
inscribed in a circle ... (57)

For Egudu this meshing of signs 'echoes the words of the Bible' and also 'mocks at the ideals they are meant to symbolize'. He is partially correct, although they are not so much a conscious attempt at parody as an apparent symbol of a present disorder and imminent new order. Since the process being undergone is not a bona fide anything, it seems to be attempting to assume/inscribe some universal symbol, one which at present appears to have no definite shape, and seems to have even less spiritual significance, 'with a hollow centre'.

The contrasting voices of 'Distances' might also be said to give this movement variation of vocal texture. On three distinct occasions one hears the voice of what must be the God figure. These utterances are italicized. In the first instance ('Distances IV') the tone of this voice is distinct from that which is first introduced within the poem. Much like a soloist's voice it is prominent and confident, and it seeks to give fuller meaning to the preceding and subsequent utterances. After the description of the enigmatic symbol 'at the archway' comes the soloist:

the only way to go
through the marble archway
to the catatonic pingpong
of the evanescent halo ... (57)

Somehow, though, Okigbo does not appear to be a composer who gives too much away. The voice of his soloist, though noticeably distinct in approach and style, is so integrally fused within the work that even though it explains some of the complexities, it still sustains the general sense of mystique introduced with the initial voices. And then again, on other occasions Okigbo's soloist might (like the chamber of 'Distances I') become more dynamically involved within the total composition by assuming a musical identity: in ('Distances I') it is the shrill voice of the descant, whilst in ('Distances IV') the soloist's voice is shifted from its accustomed straightforward purpose of lucid restatement into a more complex rendition that concludes this segment:

> *after we had formed*
> *then only the forms were formed*
> *and all the forms*
> *were formed after our forming ...* (57)

Egudu sees some similarities between this utterance and biblical language.[5] For example, he takes up the first-person-plural pronoun 'we' and alludes to the collective 'us' of Genesis chapter one, thus concluding that this voice is in another way expressing a philosophy – that it represents the 'Alpha and Omega'. Anozie believes this to be a deeper explanation of the question What is the meaning of the symbol in the white chamber (147)? For him, those objects in the chamber had only been shaped after their maker was formed, and 'they are meant to express nothing but that form'. Conversely, Anne-Marie Heywood[6] refers to the 'abnormality' of usage, the lack of 'a coherent sentence', and takes up an Edmund Leach suggestion,[7] concluding that there might be no intended meaning here: non-logicality is in itself 'part of the code'.

Whatever its truth, this enigmatic riddle is bound up with creativity, and like an improviser's innate power to continuously create, it appears to make a statement about the process of spontaneous artistic creativity. The figure at the archway is a symbol of this artistic creativity; its shape does not conform to given notions of form. But it is not meant to do so. In the same

5 Romanus Egubu, 'Okigbo's Distances: A Retreat from Christ to Idoto', *Critical Perspectives* 159.

6 Anne-Marie Heywood, 'The Ritual and the Plot: The Critic and Okigbo's *Labyrinths*', *Critical Perspectives* 214.

7 Edmund Leach, *Culture and Communication* (London: Cambridge University Press, 1976) 70–74.

way that the response to this figure is prejudiced by preconceived notions of creative order (that is, it is judged with notions of 'the Cross' in mind), a fuller appreciation of Okigbo's work might depend on one's willingness to approach it in a 'new' way, 'without passing through that process of intellectual analysis'.[8]

When the solo voice is heard for the final time in section VI, it reassumes its primary purpose as chief explicator, just before the process of 'Distances' comes to an end. This is a lucid voice which invites the acolyte to engage in the final symbolic act, a signal perhaps, as Gerald Moore suggests,[9] that the initiate is prepared to receive her embrace:

> *come into my cavern,*
> *shake the mildew from your hair;*
> *Let your ear listen:*
> *My mouth calls from a cavern ...* (59)

The background strains of inauspicious references and allusions, often to prophetic literature, are as enriching to the texture of the verse as any other motif which appears in 'Distances': 'Dan to Beersheba', 'the crucifix', 'locusts', 'abyss', 'swords', 'incense', 'censer', 'marble', 'celestial', and 'sanctuary' are some of the items from within ('Distances' I–VI) whose inclusion infuse an apocalyptic tinge. In II death is foreshadowed when personified as 'lying in ambush' and 'paring her fingernails'. Images of gloom and blood hover over and taint every scene leading up to V, where the air of the macabre is heightened by a most disturbing image of affection, betrayal, and death in 'die scar of the kiss'. These images readily surface in the nebula of evening (as in III): this is a time frame that seems perennial. In fact a sense of timelessness exists throughout, from I where a feeling of vacuity, abstraction, and endless inner spaces is introduced by the

8 Okigbo in his interview with Serumaga, 9.

9 Gerald Moore, 'Vision and Fulfillment', *Critical Perspectives* 285–286.

labyrinth symbol, to VI where it reappears as 'the orangery of immense corridors' through which the acolyte has groped for what appears to be 'several centuries'.

Okigbo's is above all a music that plays on the senses. Its creation of fantasies through synaesthesia in 'water's laughter', the 'air's marrow', and the like might border on magical realism. This usage of metaphor and the imagery it evokes defamiliarises our sensibility. It challenges the reader to consider new relations between the senses. Brathwaite's magic realism in his later collections also employs metaphors to create this effect, although it must be said that unlike Brathwaite's soundtrack Okigbo's (in 'Distances') remains unnervingly personal, seldom freeing itself from the soul, where it is sounded.

The 'catatonic ping pong' in ('Distances IV') and 'music woven into funerary rose' in ('Distances V') are a few of the literal allusions to music within this section, but they spell the dying of a practice abandoned at the end of 'Limits', where the gods 'lie in state / without the long-drum'. If this is symbolic of the need for a resuscitation of the Igbo self, then 'Distances' is an exercise in meeting this need by attempting to reconnect the initiate with his soul source and the spirit of his ancestors through the use of 'the music of the long-drums'. The music of the long-drum becomes a symbol of traditional practices, about which total acknowledgement (if not acceptance) must be confessed by the artist as a precondition for achieving a total artistic outpouring. Quite significantly, ('Distances VI') concludes with the initiate's celebratory song. If Fraser's statement about Okigbo's tone of 'rejoicing' is not necessarily true of all of 'Distances', it certainly holds true for this latter segment of ('Distances VI'), where the initiate celebrates a closer union with his soul through a medium lost within 'Limits' but regained here. He sings:

I have fed out of the drum
I have drunk out of the cymbal

I have entered your bridal
chamber; and lo,

I am the sole witness to my homecoming. (60)

CHAPTER 5

The Kamau Brathwaite Music: Ritual and Tuk Aesthetics

Kamau Brathwaite's dependence on music and musicality in the construction of his art and ideas is well known.[1] Many poets have drawn from, and in turn influenced, musical styles and genres. Okigbo's fascination with Franck's 'indifference to the laws of versification', 'personal conception', and 'complicated harmonies',[2] with Ravel's understanding of how much his instrument 'could be made to yield in the matter of allusion and suggestion',[3] and with Debussy's myriad of references[4] (all making up the impressionist style), helped him to fashion verse whose basic texture was as shadowy and watery as Ravel's 'Jeux d'eau'.

After having come into contact with the style and concerns of a musical movement, Okigbo saw how he could adapt some of their conventions to his own indigenous setting and for his own purpose. Okigbo's concern with music in the sequence 'Distances' is for the most part ornamental. His focus is not cast

1 Gordon Rohlehr, *Pathfinder* (Tunapuna: Gordon Rohlehr, 1981). Emily Allen Williams, *The Critical Response to Kamau Brathwaite* (Westport: Greenwood, 2004). Ann Reckin 'Tidalectic Lectures: Kamau Brathwaite's Prose/Poetry as Sound-Space', *Anthurium* 1, 1 fall (2003). <http://anthurium.miami.edu/volume_1/issue_1/reckin-tidalectic.htm>. Accessed Sept. 30, 2007.

2 Frits Noske, *French Song from Berlioz to Duparc* (New York: Dover Publications, 1970) 243–250.

3 Anthony Blunt, *French Art and Music Since 1500* (London: Methuen 1974) 84.

4 Blunt, *French Art* 90.

upon the music per se so much as centred on vicariously elucidating the experience of his initiate's spiritual odyssey: whereas the initiate at the beginning of the ritual process stood on one leg at the passage, indecisive and 'in silence', by a later stage in the poem he has a stronger voice. By the last section of the collection, 'Path of Thunder', the poetry reflects the presence of indigenous instruments, music, and styles. So, music comes out of Okigbo's work as a conscious symbol and companion to its ongoing quest, and when his search heightens so does the music; when the quest ends, then the music ends as well.

Music is also intimately intertwined with the idea of the spiritual and artistic odyssey in Brathwaite's poetry, though it can exist independently of his poetic quest. For Brathwaite musical sources and resources are as varied as west African rhythms, work songs, the blues, jazz, ska, and the calypso. This is widely known: the rhythm of vodun possesses 'Shepherd' and 'Wake', an infectious Afro-Caribbean Pentecostal rhetoric dominates part 1 of 'The Stone Sermon', *Mother Poem*'s 'Angel/ Engine' is built upon Baptist/'Tie Head' rhythms, 'Negus' resounds with the recursive pulse of Shango, the cadence of the sermon and testimony reverberates throughout segments of *The Arrivants*, and Anglo-Catholic ritual and music is a telling feature of Brathwaite's early poetry.

As stated before, critics have discussed aspects of music and musicality in his work. Building on accepted notions of musical reference in Brathwaite's work, I have further argued in chapter 2 of *Roots to Popular Culture* that Brathwaite's poetry reflects the creative presence of his native island's indigenous percussion band called the tuk band, which currently contains bass drum, kettle drum, timpani (or steel), and penny whistle. Its origin is considered to be in slave society, and it has an even longer African background. Numerous images of the tuk band can be seen via the Internet. Important to my project is the foregrounding of Brathwaite's work on vinyl and compact disk, and other performances such as the 1981 Michael Gilkes oral dramatization of *Mother Poem*. This chapter will usually employ Brathwaite's remastered compact-disc version of the 1960s Argo recording of *The Arrivants*. I have conducted a reading of Brathwaite's *Mother Poem* employing the tuk band as a leitmotif. I have used Brathwaite's work to help formulate a reading strategy built around an understanding of the tuk band and its potential association with other creative works and expressive art forms such as poetry, rather in the same way that Brathwaite used prose in the 1960s to help discover things about jazz, music, history, art, and culture.

Whereas critics have tended to read Okigbo's music as working its way towards a climactic crescendo of indigenous drumming,[5] thereby reflecting Okigbo's ever-increasing acceptance of his immediate national responsibility, Brathwaite's work is arguably more complex to map out, despite the fact that he, like Okigbo, has increasingly come to a fuller awareness of his immediate responsibility. In a sense, Brathwaite's poetry is a systematic engagement with the development of the individual and collective consciousness and with the sequenced soundtrack that underscores this process. His work reflects a concern with how individual characters and the community are able to work out their salvation and survival through a more or less progressive set of actions.

This chapter traces one route by which Brathwaite's early poetry can be read as a critical narrative about individual and collective spiritual journeying and the audible soundtrack that supports it. This kind of reading, like that performed by other critics, tends to give support to the presence of better-known

5 See for instance, the website to the online publication *The Complete Review* '*Labyrinths* by Christopher Okigbo', n.d. <http://www.complete-review.com/reviews/nigeria/okigbo1.htm>. Accessed Sept. 10, 2008.

musical styles in Brathwaite's work.[6] But there is also a discordant soundtrack that underscores Brathwaite's early work. Rohlehr has some time ago argued for the presence of dissonance in *The Arrivants*.[7] His reading is indeed fascinating, especially in light of the focus placed on other musical tropes such as refrain, jazz, folk, blues, rasta drums, calypso, and pan.[8] This chapter, though, will seek, especially in its latter stages, to take up my earlier suggestion about the presence of other music in Brathwaite's work.

Paying attention to the printed word as well as to technologized versions of the poetry, it will eventually go on to consider the influence and impact of tuk music – yet another strain of cultural data within Brathwaite's early work. The interposing of this new music form into the mix of criticism about Brathwaite serves to defamiliarize received opinions concerning Brathwaite's use of music (which has usually been felt to be firmly rooted in 'international' reference). This interposing is especially telling in light of the ongoing critical struggle to define the place of Caribbean-international poets in a globalized environment.

A rereading of Brathwaite's poetry from the perspective of his native culture can very well lead to the realization that his work is more firmly located in his native Barbados than current critical literature acknowledges. In the final instance, it might be concluded that the complex and compressed nature of Brathwaite's early poetry makes it an appropriate work for the performance of a 'multi-tracked'[9] analysis.

6 Maureen Warner-Lewis, *Notes to Masks* (Benin city: Ethiope Publishing, 1977) and Lloyd Brown, 'The Cyclical Vision' in his *West Indian Poetry* (Boston: Twayne Publishers, 1978) 139–158.

7 *Pathfinder*, 75–77.

8 See chapter 3 in *Pathfinder*, 'The Many-Eyed Maker' 58–108.

9 See Curwen Best, *Culture @ the Cutting Edge* (Kingston: University of the West Indies Press, 2004) 1–9.

1. Multi-tracked

I have used the term 'multi-tracked' to suggest that just as recording and production technology is built upon the capacity to capture and manipulate endless tracks of data, similar operations can be performed upon cultural data if it is digitally constituted. Cultural phenomena that come into contact with technology are especially open to a multi-tracked reading: so Brathwaite's poetry, given its range of performances, recordings, and productions, and given its employment of local, regional, and extra-regional reference, must be acknowledged as being multi-tracked: an expansive range of tracks of data constitutes the poetry. This techno-reading is especially applicable to Brathwaite's poetry, given the technological representation of its texts and its poet's continuing dependence upon new technologies: because of these facts, a multi-tracked reading is desirable. This reading is able to lock into the complex process that underscores the work's construction and to perform a range of functions, in the manner of contemporary digital tools.

This chapter therefore goes on to focus on selected poems that examine the playing out of the spiritual quest in Brathwaite's early work. The poems selected are also encoded with strains of the Brathwaite music. At first, the chapter foregrounds those poems and their musics which are generally accepted within published criticism: this section of the chapter therefore denotes a critical process of reading along the grain. Later on, the chapter briefly introduces the tuk music phenomenon and considers the effects of this Barbadian cultural influence on what is generally accepted as the Brathwaite music.

In *Mother Poem* the archetypal mother has to deal with the repercussions of rootlessness within her society. One realizes as early as the first poem 'Alpha' that the song/music is as important here as it was in the earlier collection *Masks*. She is awaiting the return of her man, who has been gone for centuries. She sits patiently and 'calls on jesus name'. The poem's creator is careful not just to report on the title of the song; he opens up the poetry to the mother's vocalizing. She sings the Christian song:

when the roll is called up yonder
when the roll is called up yonder
when the roll is called up yonder
when the roll is called up yonder i'll be there.[10]

Throughout the entire poem these familiar strains resound, becoming haunting melodies of desperation from a soul in search of solace. This type of religious song becomes an integral part of the mother's daily ritual. Somehow, though, from as early as 'Sam Lord' (much earlier in the collection) one senses that her melodies are not what one would consider to be purely Christian; and by 'Angel/Engine' you know for sure, as Shango threatens to take over:

I tek up dese days wide de Zion
we does meet tuesdee nights in de carpenter shop

praaze be to god
i hear de chapman hall preacher shout out

praaze be to god

an i hear de black wings risin

10 Edward Brathwaite, *Mother Poem* (Oxford: Oxford University Press, 1977) 5.

and i feel de black rock rock

praaze be to
praaze be to
praaze be to gg[11]

This is a moment of possession. Like Okigbo's protagonist, this is her experience with 'anaesthesia'; it brings about a 'peace fire', a moment of transformation and enlightenment. This experience and its music is what appears to have been lacking in the shallow performance of her predecessors in both *Rights of Passage* and *Islands*. Herein rests the core of Brathwaite's concern with music as agent for personal and collective change/ transformation. For him it is an integral prerequisite of spiritual ritual and spiritual and social renewal. In the opening of the collection *Masks* paramount importance was assigned to music as the medium of invocation at the beginning of time, and the ritual outlined there dramatized one route by which it was possible to attain some harmony between the uninitiated and their god. The ritual represented in *Masks* had been prescribed by tradition, and the process of its enactment had to be carried out with artistic precision. Here is the prelude to spiritual and religious ritual. Music becomes both the medium and means of worship. In the making of the drum:

First the goat
must be killed
and the skin
stretched.[12]

and the reiteration of this process at the end of this section of the poem serves to reinforce the absolute necessity of undergoing this ordered sequence of events.

11 Brathwaite, *Mother Poem* 98.
12 Edward Brathwaite, *The Arrivants* (Oxford: Oxford University Press) 94.

so the goat must be killed and its skin

stretched.[13]

Then the barrel of the drum, the two curved sticks of the drummer, and other facets are added for full musical accompaniment: which Brathwaite so carefully portrays and chants[14] at the outset of the Akan prayer 'Atumpan':

Kon kon kon kon
kun kun kun kun
Funtumi Akore
Tweneboa Akore
Tweneboa Kodia
Kodia Tweneduru[15]

In *The Music of Africa* J. H. Nketia outlines some of the functions of music within traditional African societies, and he records a point with which Brathwaite appears to be in some agreement:

> The basis of association for music making, however is usually the community, those members of the ethnic group who share a common habitat and who live some kind of corporate life based on common institutions, common local traditions, and common beliefs and values.[16]

The incidence of spirituality and community is directly proportionate, since the presence of one all but compels the presence of the other. But the loss of one also signals and foreshadows the demise of the other. So, in a world where the peoples of Africa no longer share a common habitat, nor live the same kind of corporate life based on common institutions, local traditions, and beliefs and values, a social and spiritual haemorrhage results, and herein rests their fundamental de-

13 Brathwaite, *The Arrivants* 94.
14 On the recorded version of *Masks* (ARGO 33rpm. LP Record PLP 1183 London, 1972).
15 Brathwaite, *The Arrivants* 98.
16 J. H. Nketia, *The Music of Africa* (London: Victor Gallancz, 1975) 21.

ficiency. Theirs is a separation brought about by the forces of history. One of the few links which contain the possibility of rekindling a measure of spirituality is an innate rhythm (what Brathwaite calls 'immanence'),[17] which is first noticed in 'Libation' and which resurfaces in 'The Forest', 'Limits', and at intervals throughout *Masks;* but which is in danger of being forgotten by the Omowale after his journey abroad. So when Tom remembers the music of the 'Atumpan talking' it is a signal that the link with the sunsum/soul source has not been totally severed; he plays his part in keeping it alive through memory. But he will never recreate the actual rhythm through which his race will regain their spiritual solidity: that task lies with others, who are more intuitive and artistically inclined.

In *Rights of Passage* Tom's children undergo their own ritual of sojourn. It does not appear as pious as Okigbo's in the earlier poems and in 'Distances', but for all intents and purposes it is no less symbolically representative of the spiritual quest. While their 'father/founder/flounderer' achieves his spiritual sustenance through recollections of distant lands and of the minstrel 'on the logwood stump / with the dreams of his slow guitar' (in 'Didn't He Ramble'), the nightclub music heard at the end of 'The Spades' in 'The Twist' is what Tom's children seem to hold as sacred. While some critical readings of this poem from the page have tended to describe it as sordid,[18] Brathwaite's various performances of it make it one of the most rhythmic, dynamic, intriguing, and musical of all poems within *The Arrivants*. In the Argo performance the poet captures the inflection of the music of rock and roll that is the accompaniment for this once popular dance craze:

> try to hold her, keep her under
> while the juke box hiss

17 Edward Brathwaite, *History of the Voice* (London: New Beacon Books, 1984) 19.

18 Rohlehr, *Pathfinder* 38.

twist the music out of hunger
on a night like this.[19]

The underlying danger, fear, and uncertainty about their chosen path is reinforced by the sound-image of the juke box 'hiss', clearly an allusion to the serpent in the biblical Eden. This signifies how that which had brought about the downfall of mankind returns, but this time in urban and suburban Eden. Beneath the rhythmic intrigue of the poem's soundtrack lurk the forces of evil, which have managed to captivate a people on the brink of spiritual desperation and hunger, on the precipice of another fall.

In *Islands,* 'Jah' presents selected symbols of entrapment in a rapidly changing society, where the squalid setting of the shanty town metamorphoses into the Janus-faced glamour of 'the neon lights': as 'Tear and Pear Shape' puts it, 'the winking gods of electron'. Here there is no reflective music like that which Tom recalled, because 'the land has lost the memory of the most secret places'.[20]

3. Reading within the Grain: Sound Systems in *Rights*

As noticed in the poem 'Jah', many of the titles in the work *Islands* relate to religious themes. However, the manifest rhythm of the islands is hardly deeply spiritual. The islands resonate with the self-aggrandizing strains of the colonial project. The poet therefore uses irony and other tools to help convey the complex character of post-Emancipation survival methodologies. The irony locked up within the relationship between poem title and content has a substantial showing in *Rights of Passage*

19 Brathwaite, *Arrivants* 41.
20 Rohlehr, *Pathfinder* 164.

through the poet's juxtaposition of the music of the poem's title against its actual soundtrack. The ska song 'Wings of a Dove' has to do with dreaming about reaching an ideal state, heaven; but in the poetic collection its use becomes ironic, when the dream of the new 'New World' visionary and the accompanying reggae fail to elevate themselves beyond the very terrain of earth that imprisons his imagination. In Legba 'doubt / ripples the fruit / lakes, snap-/ing the bamboo,/ crack-/ing the blue'.[21] The mood created here is one of melancholy, the blues, though it is almost devoid of the deeper spiritual significance associated with the music of blues. If anything, this melancholy borders on ennui, as suggested by the wailing bamboos. This feeling of utter helplessness comes about after the episode where 'the / sugar cane screams / swinging under the steel / cutlass',[22] suggestive of the fact that the European economic and cultural holocaust sapped a people of much of their inner music.

The poem 'Caliban' represents a distinctive type of ritualistic musical creation, that of the limbo. The accompanying soundtrack is that of calypso, if only because this is one of the dominant Caribbean forms used for the performance of the limbo dance. Brathwaite's many performances of this song-poem have also evoked the music of calypso. The limbo contortion is a symbol of the life/death voyage across the middle passage between Africa and the Caribbean. The act and its music is therefore a potentially liberating phenomenon:

> long dark night is the silence in front of me
> *limbo*
> *limbo like me*
>
> stick hit sound
> and the ship like it ready ...[23]

21 See the poem 'Legba', *Arrivants* 176.

22 Brathwaite, *Arrivants* 175.

23 Brathwaite, *Arrivants* 194.

However, as we also discover in the poem, the limbo is appropriated as a tool of capitalism, an attraction for the dollar of the curious tourist, who now also him/herself attempts to get under and to resurface in an act of sacrilegious merrymaking. The music is therefore also blotted and fails to attain its true spiritual significance.

And then there is Tizzic, the masquerader of the two nights jump-up of carnival seen in 'Tizzic'. His music is also calypso – dance calypso. He is a hard worker, an alcoholic, and a tramp who seeks solace in the driving rhythm of the islands:

For he was a slave
to drums, to flutes, brave

bass and rhythm, the jump-up saved
him from the thought of holes, damp

rain through the roof of his have-
nothing cottage; kele, kalinda-stamp,

the limbo, calypso-season camp,
these he loved best of all; the road-march tramp

down Princess Street, round Mar-
aval; Kitch, Sparrow, Dougla ... [24]

His experience is explored from an interesting perspective by the poet, who accords his experience near-equal status with that of Tom's in *Rights of Passage* and Francina's in *Islands*. Like theirs, his experience, sparked by the sound of music, reconnects his sensibility to times of the past, 'days of green unhurried growing', when he might perhaps have been better able to move to the rhythm of this music. His experience is also accorded near-religious significance:

He walked so far
on stilts of song, of masqueraded story; stars

24 Brathwaite, *Arrivants* 261.

were near. Doors of St. Peter's heaven were ajar.
Mary, Christ's Christmas mother was there

too, her sweet inclined compassion
in full view.[25]

The ritual has an entrancing effect. This is his opiate of the masses:

In such bright swinging company

he could no longer feel the cramp
of poverty's confinement, spirit's damp ...[26]

However, his invocation of and attitude to music as a temporary diversion from his attendance to his true spiritual state appears misguided, and soon the 'rhythm faltered'; and the bells of Ash Wednesday, which had summoned Okigbo's initiate to self-examination, also peel for Tizzic. However, unlike Okigbo's initiate, Tizzic hardly comes face to face with his inner self. Fearing the 'Lenten sorrows' which awaited, he preferred to remain 'Behind the masks' and therefore, 'after the bambalula bambulai he was a slave again.'[27]

In the poem 'Vèvè' Tacky appears as a direct reincarnation of Tizzic. Both are hard working, but Tacky is not the limer/slacker that Tizzic was, neither is he the reveller. Tacky's resuscitation derives from an affinity with the land, as on page 264 where we hear it is 'the bird that sings / the green that wavers, wavers wins', and this leads him to a reclaiming of ritualic allegiance with his ancestors. One feels that the poet might be proposing a compromise of the characters of Tizzic and Tacky by having juxtaposed their poems and attitudes. This is given greater credence when one examines the fact that the final poem 'Jou'vert' (which, incidentally, follows the two

25 Brathwaite, *Arrivants* 262.
26 Brathwaite, *Arrivants* 262.
27 Brathwaite, *Arrivants* 262.

pieces just discussed) takes up both the driving music of Tizzic's two nights jump-up and the deeper philosophizing in Tacky's 'Vèvè', and treats them in fusion:

> but the sorrows
> burn to ashes
>
> grey rocks
> melt to pools
>
> of lashes'
> sweat and flowers
>
> bloom along the way
>
> *bambalula bambulai*
> *bambalula bambula.* [28]

This concern with form, rhythm, and cultural aesthetics as liberating agents is also observed at the beginning of the 'Rebellion' section, where 'Wake' questions the absence of the word, of which Ananse will be creator; and it achieves fuller exploration in 'Negus', which is widely heralded as an experiment with form and rhythm.

4. Tuk Band Rhythm: Within and Against the Grain

It should be recognized that the poet imagines the folk voice as sounding the dominant register and holding the pervading cadence that supports his early poetry: hence we hear the variety of strains mentioned above. But prior to my suggestion in *Barbadian Popular Music* and *Roots to Popular Culture* that Brathwite's poetry also reveals the presence of the native Barbadian tuk style, there had been no sustained, studied

28 Brathwaite, *Arrivants* 268.

discussion about the location of this musical form and its impact on Brathwaite's work. Given the magnitude of such a topic, and also given the fact that I have already examined this notion to some degree, the remainder of our discussion here locates selected samples of this music in Brathwaite's *Arrivants* and considers (merely) how the presence of such a form might impact on the poet's discourse about individual and collective spirituality and the quest, as discussed in the preceding sections of this chapter.

My employment of tuk aesthetics requires very careful consideration if one is to apply it in broad sweeping contexts. It is perhaps more useful in this case to take up one or two of my earlier suggestions about tuk and to allow them to inform the ongoing discussion about music and mission in Brathwaite's early poetry. Critical to this attempt is the task of relating the various instruments of the tuk band to corresponding elements in Brathwaite's poetry before *Mother Poem*. Although in *Mother Poem* I distinguished between the various instruments, based on the distinction between male and female voices in the poetry, that association was admitted to be arbitrary, and bound to change as other works were examined. My application of a tuk reading to Bruce St. John's *Bumbatuk* (in the same chapter of *Roots to Popular Culture*) used the relative prominence of individual characters in the poetry to determine which instrument they represent, and was also based on an awareness of the audibility and function of the various instruments of the tuk band. This chapter will follow that methodology.

I have made the point that although there are bands similar to the tuk band within other Caribbean islands, it is the tuk band's distinctive sound and cadence that gives it its particularly Barbadian identification. Likewise, though most poems in *The Arrivants* appear to sit comfortably next to the others, there are a few of them which, like the tuk band, stand out for their distinctive employment of Brathwaite's Bajan tuk style. These poems are – significantly – also at the centre of Brathwaite's exploration of life, death, ritual, spirituality, and music. Two such poems are 'The Dust' and 'Rites', of which we will examine the former in some depth.

These two poems are built upon the Barbadian cadence: as scribal documents the poems contain some features (phonological, morpho-syntactic and lexical) of the Bajan nation language.[29] Brathwaite's own performance of these poems on the Argo recording also bears out the presence of the Barbadian sound. It is this very Barbadian sound that distinguishes these poems from others (in the same way, perhaps, that every speaker's cadence distinguishes him or her). Although the discussion here focuses principally on 'The Dust', it should be said that the marking of these poems as Bajan and as tuk poems provides an opportunity to examine where they fit within the matrix of the cultural and spiritual journey which Brathwaite's work explores.

Rohlehr is sure that he hears Eliot and his music in Brathwaite's 'The Dust', and Charles Pollard seems to concur in a more recent study.[30] They are both perceptive in this regard, since Brathwaite's poetry does indeed reflect a similar examination of the new 'New World' wasteland. But there are – inevitably – other ways of listening to Brathwaite's verse. A perception that pays closer attention to the soundscape of Brathwaite's native Barbados can very well hear a different soundtrack. A closer listen to this poem can very well reveal the overt accompaniment of tuk. Given the earlier development of tuk, its power and connection to the African past accords it a prime place in the construction of Caribbean cultural aesthetics.

29 See the description of Bajan nation language in John Roy's 'The Structure of Tense and Aspect in Barbadian English Creole' in *Focus on the Caribbean,* ed. Manfred Görlach (Philadelphia: John Benjamin Publishing, 1986) 141–156. Also see Audrey Burrowes and Richard Allsopp's 'Barbadian Creole' in *Studies in Caribbean Language,* ed. Lawrence Carrington (Cave Hill: UWI School of Education, 1983) 38–45.

30 Rohlehr, *Pathfinder* 104, also see Charles W Pollard's *New World Modernisms* (Charlottesville: Univ. of Virginia Press, 2004).

Tuk is inherently multi-layered, inherently multi-tracked. It is comprised of at least four percussive voices. This percussion-driven music, which served the function of survival and resistance in pre- and post-Emancipation society, can hardly be ignored in any exploration of the complex interrelation between economic and cultural factors in the development of Barbadian and Caribbean society.

To ignore the rhythm of tuk in this poem and to superimpose the melancholic music of the wasteland is perhaps also to lose the singsong rhythm that Brathwaite conveys so naturally in the Argo recording. The tuk performance infuses a livelier rendition: the music of tuk is inherently buoyant. The poem is therefore less bleak than Eliot's *Waste Land*. The tuk band's intricate interplay of instruments (bass drum, kettle drum, triangle/timpani, and lead penny whistle), is conveyed in the poem by the discursive nature of its dialogue and voicings: the different voices in the village shop become like different instruments of the band. The predominance of the female voice is also a crucial signifier, which reinforces the vital role of women in the formulation and deployment of survival strategies. Tuk's characteristic rising and falling of tonal and rhythmic values is also suggested in the poem by the short responses and slightly different registers of the various voices, who like their fellow 'New World' icons, discuss and play out the theme of survival, renewal, and liberation.

In the tuk band the penny whistle is the only melodic instrument. It therefore tends to lead and give direction to the band. For all intents and purposes the tuk band's lead instrument, the penny whistle, is represented in the voice of the lead speaker. In this poem Ms Olive's voice is one of the strongest. She controls the direction of the performance to a significant degree (though her voice also gives way to others at various points of the poem). The kettle drum, which is next to the penny whistle in terms of its dynamics and audibility, is represented in the voices of the various other women when they intervene in the performance. The less audible and less conspicuous role of the timpani/steel is represented by the voices which do not speak directly but which are reported within the poem: for example, the voices of Mister Gilkes and of the Pastor, who both sound warnings about an impending disaster. The bass drum, because of its underlying pulse and metrical properties within the band, is represented by the choric punctuations that characterize the poem throughout, as when there is a collective response to Miss Evvy's testimony that 'we got to thank God / fuh small mercies' (pp. 62–63):

> Amen,
> Eveie, chile.
> Amen
> Eveie, chile
>
> an' agen
> I say is Amen.

The fact that the entire performance of 'The Dust' takes place in 'de white people shop' where the performers speak in full knowledge that their voices are potent agents of subversion, makes one recall the similar subversive nature of the tuk band. Within pre- and post-Emancipation society, the band members employed some of the instruments of their masters (drums of the British marching band), but shrewdly superimposed their own African and Barbadian rhythmic and performance style. The result was, therefore, that the band became an agent for subversion, celebration, and affirmation of African-Barbadian aesthetics. But even more so, it is a symbol of the never-dying creative spirit, and ever a source of interest, intrigue, and optimism.

The poem's performance within the White man's shop and its portrayal of the cycle of hardship and the threat of destruction is a reminder that the human forces of history have co-joined to threaten the very desire to succeed among African-Barbadian and 'New World' people. The conducting of this tuk performance on the property of the White man also signals that covert resistance is ongoing: the women do not totally shut down the 'noise in de white people shop', they merely turn it down. Theirs is therefore a tactical methodology, and the tuk band is also capable of this and other kinds of intricate and strategic transformations.

All in all, the tuk performance of 'The Dust' reminds us of other musical rituals heard throughout *The Arrivants*. 'The Dust' is also about the need to understand the nature of spiritual and social injustice, and the imperative of finding a way of escape and true liberation. Like 'Wings of a Dove' the music of 'The Dust' elevates it beyond a nihilistic dirge. The music kindles and re-kindles the possibility of reconnection to the past, reconnection to one source of survival that exists as a part of memory. Like 'The Twist' the music of 'The Dust' is also potentially secular as well as spiritual; hence the admonition by one of the performers in the poem to let go of inhibitions (pp. 67–68).

'The Dust' is also somewhat different in some respects. It is much more choric than many other early poems that explore the possibility of liberation through ritual and journey. The music of 'The Dust' is more complex in terms of orchestration and the play of voices. While it is easier to detect and identify the voices in some other poems, for example the earlier poems in *Rights of Passage*, the instruments that constitute the tuk performance of 'The Dust' are not readily distinguishable. They must carefully be listened to in order to identify them, as on pages 63, 64, 65, 67, and 68. This observation is also true of the actual tuk band and its instruments. Although the theme of the performance is defined, its orchestration reveals the presence of some tension, as, for example, when some voices caution about the performance level (p. 62) and about calling the Lord's name in vain (p. 66). But the sum output of the band of women reflects an engagement with the deep philosophical and spiritual question of how and where to find salvation.

Although this tuk poem and its performance ends, as others, without fulfilling the quest for salvation, its final statement of 'Why is that? What it mean?' (p. 69), sounded together in unison, gives hope that collective performance can fuel the engine of spiritual ritual that is the prelude to full enlightenment.

Since the forces of history have made sure that there is no longer such a thing as Nketia's 'corporate life' and 'values', the several archetypes and their spiritual/cultural expression hold the potential for recreating that link broken off at the start of *Masks*. The scoring of these several song-poems and their accompanying soundtrack has also been a rewarding experience for the poet, since in many ways this has been his search as well. As with Okigbo's 'Distances', which is a microcosmic consideration with macrocosmic implications, Brathwaite's probe into the psyche of the contemporary West Indian has also been a probe within his own sensibility, and this has meant his increasing preoccupation with form. Since music has tended to be at the centre of his people's religious activity, it has meant a conscious probe into their world of contemporary sounds and rhythms. It has meant developing a keen ear for the submerged, even suppressed, melodies of spiritual ritual, and for rhythms now fused and often infused with the trappings of a 'New World' cadence and lifestyle. But there is still the audacious unaltered, unalterable haunting tones of untrammelled reveries, like those which had been encoded into Okigbo's ritual, and like that heard in the ritual-like 'ode to the past' in 'Ancestors', where the ministrant of one generation recalls the music of his ancestors:

And in the night, I listened to her singing
in a Vicks and Vapour Rub-like voice what you would call the blues

3
Come-a look
come-a look
see wha' happen

Come-a look
come-a look
see wha' happen

Sookey dead
Sookey dead
Sookey dead-o

Sookey dead
Sookey dead
Sookey dead-o.[31]

This ritualistic mass is carried over into *Mother Poem*'s Drift-word':

so she lies
mutter of echoes, folded to silence
surrounded by the multiple death of her children
surrendered to their ancient histories

their hopes walking like rain across the distant water[32]

And when you read and listen to Brathwaite's song-poetry more than thirty years on, you still hear the multi-tracked sound of an engaging, if at times complex, music.

31 Brathwaite, *Arrivants* 240.

32 Brathwaite, *Mother Poem* 114.

CHAPTER 6

'Something Like a Mass': Ritual and Ceremony in Okigbo's 'Heavensgate' and 'Limits'

In the introduction to 'Heavensgate' Christopher Okigbo provides his own synopsis of the poem when he suggests that 'Heavensgate' was originally conceived as an Easter sequence. It later grew into a ceremony, something like a mass, an offering to Idoto.[1] There can be little doubt that the major concern of 'Heavensgate' is with the spiritual awakening of the celebrant as he comes into contact with his muse. This is not to say that the ritual/quest in Okigbo's work begins at 'The Passage' and ends in 'Newcomer' in 'Heavensgate', for it is possible to conceive of all of *Labyrinths* as a ritual, as an exploration of the effects of spiritual immersion on the individual and on society. On reaching the section 'Limits' one is still aware of the impact of religious ceremony: 'Distances' explores the entrant's spiritual and artistic voyage, and 'Path of Thunder' attempts to provide a response to the problematic interface of art, commitment, and sacrifice.

Although critical appraisals like Herbert Ekwe-Ekwe's 'Christopher Okigbo and These Times'[2] provide a balanced overview of Okigbo's contribution, Okigbo's poems of war have attracted the most attention. Critics have found his later

1 Christopher Okigbo, *Labyrinths*. (London: Heinemann Educational Books, 1971) xi.

2 Herbert Ekwe-Ekwe's 'Christopher Okigbo and These Times' in *Kwenu!: Our Culture Our Future,* Wednesday May 19, 2004. <www.kwenu.com/publications/ekwe-ekwe/okigbo_times.htm>. Accessed Nov. 20, 2007.

poems much more rewarding for teasing out the significance of the relationship between the poet's work and his real-life experiences.[3] This does not signify a weakness within the collection: critics are bound to foreground Okigbo's prophetic poems. Given the fact that his earlier work is much more private and that the later poems are about national crisis and war, critics are bound to be drawn to his final words. Some of Brathwaite's collections have also attracted more criticism than others, for one reason or another. But there are few Brathwaite critics that would deny the value of less well-known poems like 'South' within Brathwaite's poetic scheme. Poets like Brathwaite and Okigbo have invested substantially in every work, and an examination of one segment of their work lends substantially to an understanding of others.

This chapter will focus on the earlier sections of *Labyrinths,* especially 'Heavensgate' and 'Limits'. It is predominantly concerned with showing one route by which it is possible to begin to interpret Okigbo's earlier poems. It does not set out to offer this interpretation as the only valuable reading of these Okigbo poems, but by way of a close reading it wants to trace the complex process that encapsulates and preoccupies Okigbo's celebrant. This chapter therefore gives additional insight into the meanings of the spiritual quest in Okigbo's poetry.

There is a substantial body of criticism that examines the ceremonial aspect of Okigbo's poetry. Anozie's references to 'ritualistic exploration' and 'mythical projection' represent one of the better-known readings of Okigbo and of his persona's undertaking in 'Heavensgate'. Udoeyop's perspective is also well received, where he concludes that 'Heavensgate' is about 'the poet's alienation from his native culture and his attempts to

3 Also see generally 'My e-conversation with Obi Nwakanma' by Nnorom Azuonye. Dec. 2002. <www.sentinelpoetry.org.uk/NnoromAzuonyeMyeConversationsWithObiNwakanma>. Accessed Oct. 7, 2008.

re-integrate with it'.[4] Izevbaye views it all as a 'longing' which ensues because 'having become initiated into the world of strangers, he has become technically a prodigal to his own'.[5] Udechukwu agrees with Anozie. For many of these critics Okigbo's modernist tendency inspires his poetry's cryptic quality and obscure allusions.

Over the years criticism has been obsessed with meaning and non-meaning in the earlier sections of *Labyrinths,* despite and because of Okigbo's declaration that he has not explicitly 'set out to communicate a meaning'[6] and his caution that 'Heavensgate' and 'Limits' were written with no 'particular message in mind'. Very recently the poet Emman Usman Shehu dismissed Okigbo's 'Heavensgate' as a poem that has no meaning beyond the first stanza: after knowing that the prodigal is standing before the goddess, what next?[7] Too often the critics have sought to dispute whether Okigbo actually set out to convey a message in his work, as though this was the only key to an analysis of Okigbo's work: ultimately such disputes end in speculation. But in the mean time, the actual substance of his work provides too vivid an experience for the reader to endlessly debate intent versus non-intent.

Most critics agree that Okigbo's protagonist is an innocent and untrained worshipper whose attitude is penitent as he goes about obtaining his surety of salvation by following his muse/goddess, the illusory embodiment of the ultimate spirit-

4 Nyong Udoeyop, 'Okigbo: A Branch of Giant Fennel' in *Critical Perspectives on Christopher Okigbo,* ed. Donatus Nwoga (Washington: Three Continents Press, 1984) 55.

5 Dan Izeybaye, 'From Reality to the Dream: The Poetry of Christopher Okigbo' in *Critical Perspectives on Christopher Okigbo* 304.

6 Christopher Okigbo in an interview with Robert Serumaga during the Commonwealth Arts Festival July, 1965.

7 Emman Usman Shehu's comments are reported and discussed in the article by Emmanuel Sule 'Literacy Language and Recent Nigerian Fiction'. Nov. 2005. <See the Website www.africanwriter.com/articles188/1>. Accessed June 10, 2008.

ual experience. This chapter, however, begins on the premise that the initiate is not as innocent as many suppose, and it therefore devotes greater attention to the actual process of the quest: it follows the development of events throughout the various stations of the celebrant's ritual. This is a valuable critical undertaking, since too often literary scholarship on Okigbo's work treats the actual text of the poetry as secondary to Okigbo's biography. This chapter does make reference to the relationship between the poetry and the poet's life, but its prime emphasis is on approaching the subject via the poetry. Much of contemporary criticism appears to have lost the art of doing some close critical reading of the primary text. Close reading, despite its well-publicized limitations, reveals itself as one of the more rewarding critical templates for analysing the work of poets like Okigbo and Brathwaite. I am not speaking here purely of a New Critical approach, one that excludes biography, history, and so on; rather I want to make the point that while some branches of postcolonial and postmodernist discourse have subordinated the primary text, giving greater prominence to the act of reading itself, there is much pleasure to be derived still from treating the work as a critical source of data.

1. At Heaven's Gate

While he discloses that he has not explicitly 'set out to convey a meaning', Okigbo admits that his 'Heavensgate' is in fact designed to dramatize his return to his responsibilities as a reincarnation of the priest of Idoto. In the introduction to the Heinemann edition of *Labyrinths* the reader is told that 'Limits" was written 'at the end of a journey of several centuries from

Nsukka to Yola in pursuit of what turned out to be an illusion.'[8] This admission speaks of his attempt to salvage his marriage. Okigbo's preface therefore helps to explain his work, but at the same time it sets up barriers, as the reader feels compelled to search for his real life in the poems. Critics have continued to vigorously pursue this type of reading, as does Okafor Dubem in *The Dance of Death: Nigerian History and Christopher Okigbo's Poetry*.[9] This is a useful approach, and, were much more available on Okigbo, it might even be more worthwhile. Still, to be truly aware of Okigbo's aesthetic creed is to realize that the intellectual bargaining over finding 'a meaning' is bound to be all but futile.

'Heavensgate' was not created with any 'particular message in mind', for in 'Heavensgate' Okigbo is not functioning through that faculty (mind). As is well known, he was working under the spell of the Impressionist composers Debussy (perhaps with Handel's 'Water Music' in mind), Franck, and Ravel. The messages of the poem are conveyed primarily through the soul. As ('Limits' XII) indicates, the poet and the poem's persona thrive within an ambience of the sublime, where the sunbird sings 'from the Limits of the dream'.[10] For Okigbo the effect gained through the senses is as important as the logical working out of a theme or a meaning. Hence the 'Newcomer' section, which symbolizes a new birth, a new way of seeing (and yet not seeing but feeling), ends with the slightly crazed image of the entrant:

> Listening to the laughter of waters
> that do not know why:

8 Okigbo, *Labyrinths* xi.

9 Okafor Dubem in *The Dance of Death: Nigerian History and Christopher Okigbo's Poetry* (Trenton: Africa World Press, 1998).

10 Okigbo, *Labyrinths* 35.

Listening to incense –
I am standing above the noontide

with my head above it ...[11]

It is the nature of the poem's allusion (to religious worship) and its weaving and interweaving of the senses that gives it its power. The imagery of 'listening to incense' in particular encapsulates the complex responses that are produced by the poem. Such imagery takes his poetry beyond the mundane level of the intellect and logic, and unites auditory and olfactory faculties in a moment of spiritual sublimity. This has the effect of conveying the impact of the experience on the inner self, on the soul.

When one first sees the celebrant in 'The Passage' he is reciting what must be a propitiatory supplication to his deity. From the outset one senses the nature of his trials, and from where they emanate. There appears to be much anguish on his part, his cry emanates from a soul submerged in waters of turmoil, within an abyss. Although the reader senses a measure of pain, there is also a hint of self-awareness or even latent self-confidence within the sequence 'The Passage'. Yes, the reader knows that the persona's opening recitation is an invocation, but how much of it is submissive? How much of it is said with a sense of foreknowlege, anticipation, even arrogance? Need the initiate remind his goddess that he is 'lost in [her] legend'? Despite being 'lost', he so readily seems to know his way about in this world of ritual that the reader begins to suspect that the entrant has been here before. In much the same way that for him the rays 'violet and short' foreshadow the fire that is dreamed of, likewise he is aware of the imminent rains as he predicts the play of 'rain and sun in single combat'.[12]

Because he is not a total novice to this spiritual experience he seems to know that this conflict is pending. He had gone

11 Okigbo, *Labyrinths* 19.
12 Okigbo, *Labyrinths* 4.

through this kind of process before, when his grandfather died and he had had to take on greater responsibility: he is again the prodigal. In many ways he has invited this conflict upon himself, for what he is attempting throughout this process of cleansing, crystallizing, is the problematic reconciliation of two traditions, two orders, the beliefs of two worlds, so that in effect the poem might be read (at one level) as a spiritual projection of sociocultural concerns. The poem dramatizes the persona's internal struggle to reconcile traditional and Western belief systems and cultural practices. In the poem traditional values are characterized by Mother Idoto's religion, and nontraditional precepts are symbolized by Judaeo-Christian liturgy. At the most private and personal level, Okigbo's dilemma had always been whether he should side with his maternal grandfather, who had been the priest of the deity at the Ajani shrine, or with his father, the Catholic schoolteacher under whose guidance Christopher had been baptized into the Catholic faith. As a maturing artist in a growing independent nation he realized the macrocosmic signification of the microcosmic insurrections within his soul, and he dared to dramatize them.

The celebrant in 'Heavensgate' knows the world into which he has implanted himself. His encounter with the watermaid is hardly bizarre to him. He knows her and she him. What he does not know, however, is how this process is going to change his relationship with her, how different the process will be now that he has returned. If the celebrant has fooled some of the 'early' critics of 'Heavensgate' with respect to his innocence, he cannot do the same to the Imo Miri. Thus his undertaking will be arduous. In an essay on 'The Dramatic Limits of Igbo Ritual' Echeruo makes a comparative statement about the Igbo that 'they have a keen sense of stylized representational action, and ... they certainly do not lack a feeling for ceremony.'[13] This

13 Michael Echeruo, 'The Dramatic Limits of Igbo Ritual', *Critical Perspectives on Nigerian Literatures*, ed. Bernth Lindfors (Washington: Three Continents Press, 1976) 76.

observation helps one to understand and appreciate to some degree the nature of Okigbo's stylized response in the earlier sections of *Labyrinths*. It also begins to explain the near-arrogant stance that his entrant assumes. He can in no way be described as the truly penitent prodigal who seeks reconciliation with his lord/lady at his own expense, like the Christian Prodigal archetype of the New Testament. The Christian archetype comes to self-realization after a period of lavish living, and vice, in a far country. After a period of alienation both from his new lifestyle and from his self he acknowledges where he has erred, and he envisages reconciliation with his father, and under the father's conditions:

> And when he came to himself he said, How many hired servants of my father's have bread enough and to spare and I perish with hunger! I will arise and go to my father and will say unto him, Father, I have sinned against heaven, and before thee, And am no more worthy to be called thy son: make me as one of thy hired servants.[14]

Okigbo's celebrant who had first approached Mother Idoto is not the same soul as he who now approaches her in 'The Passage'. Though both know fear, the former's was born of sheer innocence, while this one's is driven by anxiety. Like the 'young bird' at a crossroads, the entrant in 'The Passage' assumes a stance of uncertainty, that of the traditional wise chicken (alluded to by Udechukwu)[15] who, on going into a new environment, assumes this stance until the inhabitants of that new world stand on both legs, whereupon he follows suit. In *Tradition the Writer and Society* Wilson Harris sees this type of process as coming to fruition when inner and outer life become one, as for a vodun dancer in a trance.[16] Okigbo's celebrant is

14 *Holy Bible* King James Version, St. Luke chap. 15 vs. 17–19.

15 Obiora Udechukwu, 'Aesthetics and the Mythic Imagination', *Critical Perspectives on Christopher Okigbo* 80.

16 Wilson Harris, *Tradition the Writer and Society* (London: New Beacon, 1967) 51.

perfectly familiar with and assumes all the ritualistic stances, but until he is willing to offer up his inner life for worship his quest can only be 'something like a mass'.

In II ('Initiations') the persona's voice returns to the early stage of childhood innocence to rescue early experiences and juxtapose them with more recent events, 'united in vision / of present and future'. This is somewhat reminiscent of Kamau Brathwaite's undertaking, especially within his first trilogy and the early works of the second trilogy, where he explores the various influences of school, church, plantocracy, and vernacular culture on the individual's psyche. In *Mother Poem*, for instance, the son comes under the tutelage of the colonial education system. He is at the mercy of Chalkstick the teacher, whose task is to teach the boy how to forget the drum and African history. Much earlier, at the beginning of *Rights of Passage* it is Tom who recognizes the importance of schooling and education in the formation of the mind. Brathwaite, like other Caribbean writers of his generation, has paid substantial attention to this thematic construct, and in *Labyrinths* Okigbo also attempts to understand how the first experience of schooling can shape the individual's spiritual and religious orientation. On reflection, the weight of Christian teaching is substantial, though its outcomes are indeterminate:

> so comes John the Baptist
> with bowl of salt water
> preaching the gambit:
> life without sin, without
>
> life; which accepted,
> way leads downward
> down orthocenter
> avoiding decisions.[17]

17 Okigbo, *Labyrinths* 6.

The entrant of 'Heavensgate' is a pupil of such schooling. Being vulnerable to John's baptism (which he has accepted) leads to vacillation and his 'avoiding decisions', the effect of which is reflected in the vision of the young bird at a crossroads in 'The Passage'. A main source of his dilemma therefore stems from the discomfort that his institutionalization engenders. The 'obligation' to such a life for him presages an existence that either makes of him 'the square' and 'yields the moron' or merely alters his disposition ('the rhombus') while he remains unchanged, like 'selfish selfseekers / - all who are good / doing nothing at all'.[18]

One feels that the celebrant is resentful of such a restricting lifestyle because he has had to suffer under the hand 'that wielded the blade'. But although he is critical of those positions and angles taken, he does not appear at that stage of his life to have worked out alternative angles or alternative models. Even now, on reflection, he is left in solitude, indecisive and with only latent memories about the childhood process of being schooled. As he contemplates the past other teachers appear, Jadum and Upandru. Jadum, 'the half-demented village minstrel' (as Okigbo tells us), is the prescriptive teacher whose bardic aphorisms are too rhetorical, and seemingly of little relevance to actual childhood development. Upandru, 'a village explainer' is also given to teaching by way of a form of proverb, but his call-and-response type discourse makes his lessons more worthwhile. His catechism leads to the question, the proverb: 'Except by rooting, / who could pluck yam tubers from their base'?[19]

Herein is the source of the celebrant's plight. A panacea lies within the root. The secrets that are hidden, those 'bedchamber thoughts' within the 'mind-window', must be rooted out and confessed in Idoto's watery presence before any meaningful

18 Okigbo, *Labyrinths* 7.
19 Okigbo, *Labyrinths* 9.

spiritual connection can be forged. This constitutes the inner life to which Harris was referring, that half which must be given over along with the outer life as a precondition to affirmation and possession.

In III ('Watermaid') the persona secretly tells what we are meant to believe is the true state of his soul ('secret I have told into no ear / save into a dughole'). Because of his muted uttering/ offering he only manages a brief moment of detached contact with the muse:

> maid of the salt-emptiness,
> sophisticreamy ...
>
> BRIGHT
> with the armpit-dazzle of a lioness ...
>
> So brief her presence –
> match-flame in wind's breath –[20]

His detached honesty is matched by her response. She hardly allows him to capture her presence. He therefore feels unfulfilled, abandoned:

> AND I WHO am here abandoned,
>
> count the sand by wavelash abandoned,
> count her blessing, my white queen.[21]

When we come to 'Lustra' we hear the entrant's intention conveyed in such phrases as 'so would I ...', which sounds more like a dilating ambition than a penitent confession. He dreams about a return 'for the cleansing', and considers his spiritual condition 'as a new laid egg', to be ripe for the breaking. A form of sacrament is administered, and a parallel is drawn between his return (reconciliation) and Christ's second coming; this manifests itself through the syncretism of traditional and Western

20 Okigbo, *Labyrinths* 10, 11.
21 Okigbo, *Labyrinths* 12.

religious forms symbolized in the allusions to Milton's *Paradise Lost* and to the traditional Igbo 'palm grove' ritual. This constitutes a restatement of his deepest concern, which has to do with reconciling his soul's contradictions. But his reiterative incantations can do little if on every occasion of this quinquennial sacrifice he merely involves himself in ritualistic practice. The final step of the purification presents his obsession with reconciling the conflict of his soul, but it reveals his concern only as an obsession of the mind and not of the heart. His final rite is one befitting royalty, one whose 'thundering drums and cannons' is a celebration of the possibilities of traditional and colonial forms of enactment when 'the spirit is in the ascent'.

If 'Lustra' concludes with a resounding degree of success, accomplishment, and celebration, then section V ('Newcomer') begins in direct contrast. In this section of the newcomer's first worship session, syncretism is still his objective practice; but his own soul seems to lack the spirit of trust, confidence, and commitment which are defining attitudes of worship: 'Time for worship'.[22] This is his call to worship: it endeavours to be affirmative and to convey a sense of urgency, but it is too detached and ostentatious, and does not engender an atmosphere of worship. His call stops just short of being ritualistic regurgitation. The tonal disparity between this laconic monotone and the subsequent euphonious voice of the entrant reveals the distance between the ostentatious language of soulless ritual and the inner language of the soul:

> Time for worship-
> softly sing the bells of exile,
> the angelus,
> softly sings my guardian angel.

He does not stay in the true attitude of worship, but soon loses his interest. His making the sign of the Cross appears even

22 Okigbo, *Labyrinths* 17.

more pretentious and sacrilegious when he mouths a prayer charged with less than pious supplications:

Anna of the panel oblongs,
protect me
from them f--- angels;
protect me
my sandhouse and bones.[23]

The similarities between this supplication and that first heard in 'The Passage' are evident: both are seeking some form of providence and spiritual fulfillment, but neither is convincing as a sincere religious offering. The reception that this new child gains must perforce be cold and synthetic, for the reactions given in this world are a reflection of one's own inner state. So there can be nothing definite about the process which ends here: on the one hand there is the joy of standing above the noon tide, but concomitantly there is fear of sinking feet – 'the waters / tide blows them under'.[24]

2. Beyond 'Limits'

When the new section 'Siren Limits' is introduced the entrant's attitude is little changed from that manifested within the previous poem 'Newcomer'. The celebrant is still not submissive and appears even more prone than before to lust and concupiscence ('the he goat on heat'): yet he is quick to declare that he has had his cleansing. This is quite premature, for he must first make contact with his inner inhibitions and fears, and it is not until the subsequent sequence ('Limits' II) that he begins to do

23 Okigbo, *Labyrinths* 17.
24 Okigbo, *Labyrinths* 19.

so. Here the persona's tone shifts somewhat, becoming a bit more pensive as the clue to the gateway through the labyrinth (which was first overheard in the conversation between the initiate and the village explainer Upandru) is verbalized once more:

> FOR HE WAS a shrub among the poplars,
> Needing more roots
> More sap to grow to sunlight,
> Thirsting for sunlight ...[25]

For the first time, verbal advances are not directed externally. There is now a preoccupation with the inner state of being/'the selves', as the initiate looks 'into the soul'. For the first time in all of *Labyrinths* the initiate begins to exude honesty as he declares the extent of his unpreparedness: '& the mortar is not yet dry'.[26] He realizes with his torn heart that there is no easy pathway to resolution, restoration, or restitution: 'and this is the crisis point'. Then in the latter half of ('Limits' III) he bares his soul. This is reflected by his abandonment of his inner self to the rhythmic spontaneity that can often lead to regeneration. The pulse of this section is defined by bouts of tension and release. The entrant pauses, offers his undammed soul, and the rushing waters of Idoto rise in a litany of unprecedented honesty. It is significant at this time that the poem employs parallelism, a structural feature often associated with the traditional African panegyric:

> Hurry on down –
>   Thro' the high-arched gate –
> Hurry on down
>   little stream to the lake;
>
> Hurry on down
>   Thro' the cinder market –

25 Okigbo, *Labyrinths* 24.
26 Okigbo, *Labyrinths* 25.

Hurry on down
    in the wake of the dream ...[27]

Since he has now attempted to approach his goddess without inhibitions, his reward is pending: for after this inward reach he is taken to another realm. His lady's touch that had left a scar of the crucifix over his breast in 'Initiations' now leaves 'not ... a mark'. The worshipper is now ready to undertake this traditional quinquennial pilgrimage to the sacred waterfall. Now the watermaid's stay is more sustained and rewarding than in III ('Watermaid'), hence the more detailed descriptions of ('Limits' IV). At this point the goddess seems prepared to deal with the entrant as worshipper. As a penitent worshipper he will find his goddess to be less physically appealing ('oblong headed'). He will discover that she is capable of inflicting punishment, especially given the protracted nature of his estrangement. His woeful preamble to this re-initiation will weigh heavily against him: his chastening will be severe. He knows that inevitably he must pay for his soul's delinquency. Like the Christian archetype the Prodigal Son, he is now willing to accept the worst. In a half sleep he utters:

Wound me, O sea-weed ...

When you have finished
& done up my stitches,
Wake me near the altar,
& this poem will be finished ...[28]

He had foreshadowed this moment of sacrificial penitence to Upandru when he recited the Igbo proverb: 'Except by rooting, / who could pluck yam tubers from their base'?[29]

'Fragments' dramatizes the possibility of restoration. There is both inner and outer harmony. The initiate begins a vigil as

27 Okigbo, *Labyrinths* 26.
28 Okigbo, *Labyrinths* 27.
29 Okigbo, *Labyrinths* 9.

he prepares for a pilgrimage, taking on his Cross of iron in sections VI and VII.[30] Like all pilgrimages this one will be fraught with passion and pain. Section VIII represents the initiate as a sunbird who must negotiate his way past ominous-looking birds of prey. Nwoga agrees that these are symbols of 'colonial missionary and economic exploitation'.[30] There is a sense of inevitability about this encounter, for what could have been done to stop this? The blind dog's howl foreshadows the initiate's nurse's fear that she has lost him to other forces. But it is not her loss alone, for ('Limits' X) recasts this as the rape of an entire civilization, exemplified in the violation of the 'twin-gods of Irkalla'.

At this moment of great loss of traditional values, when his people's religious practices are denigrated, there is cosmic disquiet. Thus in ('Limits' XI) the gods lie in state but without the 'long-drum', the traditional symbol of life. The problem is not so much that the gods are no longer there, rather that the medium for invoking their presence (the drum) is no longer present. The drum would more readily have been disposed of by the colonial forces than would any other indigenous sacred cultural possession. The gods' lying in state is a symbolic allusion to their death – they are mere showpieces that have little significance beyond that of anthropological relics. In Brathwaite's work ancestral relics and the drum are also signifiers of power. In the collection *Masks* he opens the work with images of the drum under construction. Because many of the New World Africans of Tom's generation do not remember their gods intimately, their children are in danger of total estrangement. Reconnection is needed; hence Tom's many supplications.

In ('Limits' XII) a type of rediscovery – an unearthing, an uprooting – takes place, and it does so 'at the window', the 'mind-window' of 'Initiations'. This is not the type of revolu-

30 Donatus Nwoga, 'Okigbo's Limits: An Approach to Meaning', *Critical Perspectives on Christopher Okigbo* 100–101.

tionary awakening which would radically overturn the tide of European dogma; rather it is a voice barely audible at the 'off side of a dream remembered'. This is only the echo of a subsequent revolution. The sunbird, the symbol of the Igbo spirit, is not dead but lives 'where the caress does not reach'; that is, within the heart. The voices of the folk sing again: they sing of the pogrom of Igbo spiritual values. Like Picasso's *Guernica*, the harm done to such souls as Okigbo's initiate is tantamount to the bloody violation of an entire culture and race. These scars that are inflicted never really disappear, but remain within the heart, soul, and psyche of all those who survive the process of spiritual and cultural violation. Where in ('Limits' XII) the initiate would renew his soul's commitment to his goddess by singing again, his strains are affected. They resound with the disturbing melodies of an affected heart, a wandering soul, and infected tongue: 'The slits of his tongue / cling to glue'.[31]

Okigbo's 'Heavensgate' and 'Limits' are an exercise in reconciling the antagonism that was brought on by Europe's domination of Africa, and by Africa's too facile 'abandonment' ('Limits' XI) of some of their traditional customs. Although Beier might be partially correct when he suggests that Okigbo's depersonalizing his poem throws 'a veil' over its 'immediate meaning',[32] the depersonalization has an effect of giving the poem broader national and even universal levels of interpretation.[33] The private voice heard throughout the stations of Okigbo's undertaking is a symbolic voice, none the less: it is archetypal. Okigbo equates his initiate to Gilgamesh, but he is also Igbo, Nigerian, west African. He might also be seen to resurface in Brathwaite's work. He is not unlike Brathwaite's Omowale discussed in the following chapter. He is any human

31 Okigbo, *Labyrinths* 35.

32 Ulli Beier, Review of Heavensgate in 'Three Mbari Poets' *Critical Perspectives on Christopher Okigbo* 43.

33 See 'Postcolonial Generations: Yeats and Okigbo', Alex Irvine. n.d. <http://alexirvine.net/okigbo.pdf>. Accessed July 21, 2007.

being who has to struggle with the contradictions brought on by cultural penetration. As Okigbo remarked to Marjory Whitelaw: 'I believe that any writer who attempts a type of inward exploration will in fact be exploring his own society indirectly. Because the writer isn't living in isolation'.[34]

34 Christopher Okigbo in an interview with Marjory Whitelaw, 1965.

CHAPTER 7

'I Could Not Hear The Drum': *Masks* and the Importance of Return

Okigbo's initiate was seen harbouring a feeling of spiritual guilt before his native goddess, a guilt that resulted in his inability to candidly present himself and his condition to her. The condition of humiliation arising from colonialism is also treated in West Indian verse. Okigbo's initiate needed to return to his folk origins, his source of religious beginning ('except by rooting') as a starting point towards reaching a resolution and achieving a measure of spiritual equilibrium. *Masks* is in a way Brathwaite's attempt to come to grips with his origins. It is his first major poetic collection to undertake this project. A return to the time of 'innocence', to one's roots, holds more possibilities for cleansing than any other single process or undertaking can claim. This reconnection with his roots is partly a symbolic act: it is partly a formal undertaking. It is also a personal act: it is personal for the poet, yet it has wider significance, since the poet would have us consider the meaning, importance, and necessity of such an undertaking. This return has to come about because the West Indian seen in *Mother Poem* and other collections is caught up in a clutter of religious, cultural, and other rituals, equally as confusing as that in which Okigbo's entrant found himself.

Mother Poem and other subsequent collections that dramatize the lifestyle of the Caribbean slave and his descendents reflect the presence of Western- and African-style religious practices. Elsewhere Brathwaite has spoken about the interlocking influence of religious practices that thrive in the West Indies,[1] which he has tended to read as a potentially positive phenomenon. But his poetic work also foregrounds the tensions that are at work within the consciousness of his characters because of the competing cultural and religious systems. If his poetry suggests that the Caribbean is defined by the presence of a range of contributing cultures and civilizations, his work also acknowledges the need to come to terms with the various contributing strains. If *X/Self* and later collections pay attention to many more of the contributing tracks, *Masks* represents a starting point for the poet in a project that has personal, symbolic, and real objectives.

In *Mother Poem*'s 'Angel/Engine' Brathwaite captures the moment of interface between Pentecostalism and Shango. As the mother goes about trying to 'keep her body and soul seem together' she resorts to religion for support and some stability. Her religion helps her, but it too is undergoing a process of dynamic movement. She begins by confiding in the Parson and a brand of Euro-Catholic liturgy, but eventually she resorts to the more vibrant local assembly. It is Pentecostal and Christian, but also Shango when the overpowering sounds of worship reverberate:

praaaze be to
praaaze be to
praaaze be to gg ...

praaaze be to
praaaze be to
praaaze be to sh ...

praaaze be to
praaaze be to
praaaze be to

ssssssssssssssshhhhhhhhhh[2]

1 Kamau Brathwaite in an interview with the Caribbean Broadcasting Corporation (CBC), Barbados, 1987.

2 Edward Brathwaite, *Mother Poem* (Oxford: Oxford University Press, 1977) 98–103.

This moment of fusion reflects one of the more memorable experiences for the mother. It reflects her (and part of her society's) reconnection with their spiritual and cultural roots. But collections like *Mother Poem* do not simply dramatize and romanticize this process, as though reconnection is an easy undertaking. Indeed, part of the complexity of the movement towards self and collective spiritual affirmation has to do with negotiating other types of influences. One of the more compelling challenges to this process of negotiation revolves around the infiltration of corruption and secularization.

The poem 'Sam Lord', partly a satire of established religion, takes the Twenty-third Psalm and alters its subject matter by including aspects of indigenous Barbadian culture, folklore, and place names:

> The Lord is my shepherd
> he created my black belly sheep
>
> he maketh me to lie down in green pastures
> where the spiders sleep
>
> he leadeth me beside the still waters
> lakes, green pond, constitution river, glitter bay ...[3]

When this poem is read along with other tracks of experience to do with the corruption practised by the Parson and his brand of religion, it signals the extent to which religion has had to become deformalized to free it from a certain geocultural anchor. This version of Psalm 23 is the mother's version. To some it might seem a sacrilegious act, but it is also potentially an act to allow the ritual of established liturgy to bear the burden of her real-life experience. Here is a poetic rendition that on one level might appear humorous, yet is also a serious attempt to give perspective to and to localize an otherwise hollow ritualistic supplication, as taught by the Parson and his denomination. Poems such as 'Bell' (*Mother Poem*), with its muddle of spiritual,

3 Brathwaite, *Mother Poem* 8.

paternal, and emotional allegiances to the Parson, to spiritual propriety and formality on the one hand, and to the inner desire for change and redress on the other, are an indication of the degree of resentment which the emerging Caribbean citizen harbours towards a spiritually repressive social system. Thus in 'Bell' the Mother is caught apologizing to the Parson for conditions that have been inflicted upon her:

an I did love him so
                forgive me, father

the merchant own me husband
an me husband never home

                forgive me, father ...[4]

1. Masking Sound

When we hear Brathwaite's initiate in *Masks*, therefore, he is attempting to save his children from the types of dilemma seen in *Mother Poem*. But events would not be kind to him. Brathwaite's Caribbean subjects are therefore constantly under pressure to define a place of solace, a place where they have some relative peace of mind, body, and spirit. Mark McWatt puts this quite lucidly when he says that 'Brathwaite is concerned therefore with the rediscovery of an African past and identity that will remove from the black man of the New World the sense of "loss" and dereliction.'[5] The process of libation within traditional west African religion is always a meticulous undertaking and

4 Brathwaite, *Mother Poem* 12.

5 Mark McWatt, 'The Two Faces of El Dorado: Contrasting Attitudes Towards History and Identity in West Indian Literature', *Proceedings of the IVth Annual Conference on West Indian Literature,* ed. Mark McWatt (Barbados: U.W.I Cave Hill, 1985) 43.

cannot be performed without a strict adherence to ritualistic principles. Okigbo's initiate had to address Mother Idoto as a prelude to presenting any sacrificial offerings. Brathwaite's Omowale (prodigal son) in *Masks* must also pay homage to tradition in 'The Making of the Drum':

I

The Skin

First the goat
must be killed
and the skin
stretched.[6]

Then the barrel of the drum is made:

For this we choose
wood of the *tweneduru* tree:
hard *duru* wood
with the hollow blood
that makes a womb.[7]

The idiophones (according to Nketia) – the curved sticks of the drummer, gourds and rattles, and the gong-gong are the final components:

God is dumb
until the drum
speaks.

The drum
is dumb
until the gong-gong leads

it[8]

6 Edward Brathwaite, *The Arrivants* (Oxford: Oxford University Press, 1973) 94.
7 Brathwaite, *The Arrivants* 95.
8 Brathwaite, *The Arrivants* 97.

It is only after the symbolic drum is constructed that the initiate can address his higher power as Asase yaa (the Akan Earth Goddess), and with full musical accompaniment:

we are addressing you
ye re kyere wo

we are addressing you
ye re kyere wo

listen
let us succeed

listen
may we succeed ...[9]

What follows thereafter, from 'Path-Finders' to 'Arrival', is as much an exploration of the spiritual cycle of west African society as an examination of its political and geopolitical altercations. Okigbo tended to perceive the forces of opposition as predators ('eagles', 'beaks of bronze') which were in direct conflict with the sunbird. Such forces do intervene in *Masks* as well, for in 'Sunsum' the battle of religions is relived:

I remember so well ?
Why did our gold, the sun's
sunsum, safe against termites, crack

under the white gun
of plunder, bright bridge-
head of money, quick bullet's bribe?

Why did the god's
stool you gave us,
Anokye,

not save us from pride,
foreign tribes' bibles,
the Christian god's hunger.[10]

9 Brathwaite, *The Arrivants* 99.
10 Brathwaite, *The Arrivants* 149.

Masks becomes so concerned with the ritual of life and death that it is impossible not to perceive it as a religious cycle. The journey motif is overpowering: it echoes the Israelites' sojourn in the wilderness. Brathwaite has alluded to this similarity by re-emphasizing the condition of leaderlessness first introduced at the beginning of *Rights of Passage* in the epigraph taken from the biblical book of Exodus.

In the same way that an abdication of religious duty was responsible for the spiritual loss and subsequent labyrinthine quest of 'Heavensgate', the religious leaders and El Hassan the son of Amida, seen in 'The Golden Stool' and 'Axum' respectively, are equally guilty of this greatest of sins. They are responsible for the 'hacked heart' which the soul-source of 'Sunsum' experiences. In a panegyric to himself El Hassan boasts about the cruelty of his exploits against this very soul source:

> I, El Hassan, son of Amida,
> King of Axum ...
>
> made war on the Noba ...
>
> burnt town, destroyed villages,
> pillaging
>
> houses and temples ...[11]

His has been an act of desecration, which has served to undermine his position as political, moral, and spiritual leader ('pillaging houses and temples'). Still, at the root of this crisis of spiritual loss must be the incredible behaviour of the priestly sect, who lose all sense of tradition and duty in the face of a growing materialism:

> For the tribe's
> sake, the priests cried:
>
> die: for the Stool's

11 Brathwaite, *The Arrivants* 103.

honour, shrine's wealth,

lean slaver's health of
money.[12]

So scandalous have been the goings-on during the process of sojourn that the Omowale, he who had journeyed even further abroad to return transformed, now cannot respond to the affirmation of the talking drums first heard in 'Atumpan'. 'The New Ships' portrays this prodigal in a catechism with the ancestors similar to Okigbo's with Upandru: 'do you remember?'. Like the initiate of 'Heavensgate' he is forced to verbalize his inner silences:

I tossed my net
but the net caught
no fish

I dipped a wish
but the well
was dry

beware
beware
beware

I travelled to a distant town
I could not find my mother
I could not find my father
I could not hear the drum[13]

One remembers it is in ('Limits' XI) where:

AND THE gods lie in state
And the gods lie in state
Without the long-drum.[14]

12 Brathwaite, *The Arrivants* 145.
13 Brathwaite, *The Arrivants* 125.
14 Okigbo, *Labyrinths* (London: Heinemann Educational Books, 1971) 34.

This kind of indifference to the drum in *Masks*, which signifies a spiritual deafness and cultural death, has meant that the Omowale cannot sing responses to the many calls made upon him. It was also with much pain that Okigbo's initiate in ('Limits' XIII) struggled to 'sing in shadows, wobbling under [his] bones'. But like the sunbird of ('Limits' XII) that rises like a phoenix, the Omowale senses that arrival is imminent when he concludes the 'Crossing The River' section with:

For I am the life of my people.
Like the cock
I produce stocks
of life
like the hen
I bear eggs when
the cycle is ripe ...[15]

In 'Heavensgate' the initiate's plight is unmitigatedly religious/ spiritual, and in *Masks* the greater quest is likewise a spiritual one. But there is also a concern with an underlying streak of secularism that begins here in Africa and expands throughout the *Rights of Passage* sequences. This secular streak is first introduced with 'the tribes' and later explored in the journeys of Tom's progeny in the West. In this respect it is significant that Nketia speaks of three modes of drumming which he hears in *Masks*; these, he emphasizes, create poetry that is at once secular and religious.

In Brathwaite's judgement the black man's odyssey was initially born of a need for spiritual and cultural grounding:

I have longed for

markets again, for parks
where my people may walk,
for homes where they may sleep,
for lively arenas

15 Brathwaite, *The Arrivants* 146.

where they may drum and dance.
Like all of you I have loved
these things, like you
I have wanted these things.[16]

However, with the passing of time spiritual exile manifests itself in a number of ways, impacting all spheres of human endeavour and blurring the root cause of their exile. Whereas it is the system's disruption (seen in 'Ougadougou') that spurs migratory wandering, it is a festering disenchantment and disillusionment that fuels the timeless trek thereafter and within *Rights of Passage*.

In the section 'Path-Finders' an otherwise spiritual journey is converted into meaningless sojourn as the tribe moves with the stately pace of 'Mmenson' through 'Ougadougou', 'Chad', and 'Timbuctu' to 'Volta', where the plea 'have we not travelled enough?' brings temporary respite, and a brief uplifting of the soul: but this is short-lived, and by 'Techiman' 'the path through gloom' lays before them once more, up to the end of 'Crossing the River'. Throughout this movement the initial spiritual purpose becomes lost as these sojourners come to perceive their wandering less as a spiritual quest and more as a political and social condition; and so they approach it with an air of mundane indifference.

Their heirs in *Rights of Passage* are not dissimilar to the wanderers seen in *Masks*. Tom's progeny are the men of the world. Their journey, now the anti-quest, takes them to all quarters of the globe:

And so it was Little
Rock, Dall-
as, New Orleans, Santiago
De Cuba, the miles
of unfortunate islands ...[17]

16 Brathwaite, *The Arrivants* 107–108.
17 Brathwaite, *The Arrivants* 36.

They go to New York, Harlem, Paris, Switzerland, and even to Texas where their 'zoot suits' and the 'bright bold cash' are symbols of their new lifestyle. The twist, that dance craze of the 1960s, embodies their artistic potential. It is transformed into a sordid rite in the poem of the same name. The manipulation of its rhythm and rhyme scheme serves to punctuate its sensual entanglement. The serpentine imagery foreshadows the potentially dangerous consequences that lurk beneath the insatiable desire for casual pleasure:

> try to hold her, keep her under
> while the juke box hiss
> twist the music out of hunger
> on a night like this.[18]

The cyclical movement is carried on within 'Folkways', which resounds with the audible choo-chooing of a train's engine and takes on an hypnotic sound, echoing the protracted wandering of a generation:

> come quick
> bugle
> train, quick
> quick bugle
> train, black
> boogie
> woogie wheels
> fat
> boogie-
> woogie waggons
> rat tat tat ...[19]

Brathwaite's insight that the god Shango has possessed the engine/locomotive in the New World makes the inclusion of 'Folkways' into this discussion on spirituality even more valid

18 Brathwaite, *The Arrivants* 41.
19 Brathwaite, *The Arrivants* 33.

and revelatory. Its inclusion therefore signals that all is not lost; there is still a possibility of redemption. Although Tom's children are part of a lost generation, they are not totally cut off from the subterranean soul source. They still have agency, they can make critical choices of the soul.

The imposed rigours of a changed and changing society had also presented Okigbo's archetypal ministrant with the dangerous choice of leaving off his spiritual calling (his duty to Idoto) in search of another order (a growing interest in scholarship and business), and he had spent some time as a prodigal. But through the process of memory he had sought to reconcile and to reunite the former and the latter self. It is voices like those heard in 'Volta'[20] which are also constant reminders to the tribe of their true devotion. Brathwaite reinforces the conflict between ritual as spiritual and secular process by constantly and consciously juxtaposing those voices and those characters that are devotees of the two separate processes. Amidst the hollow lifestyles of a materialist society there is a voice like Tom's, which calls his children to remembrance of

> Atumpan talking and the harvest branch-
> es, all the tribes of Ashanti dreaming the dream
> of Tutu, Anokye and the Golden Stool ...[21]

In 'South' and 'The Cabin' similar voices admonish their peers to reorient and reconnect with a higher mission, in the process ascribing equilibrium to an otherwise indifferent race.

Brathwaite's concern with journeying, beginning in *Masks*, has purported to be as candid as Okigbo's had been in 'Heavensgate' and 'Limits': hence there are no easy solutions. This poetry does not present a utopian climax. Instead it is defined by its dramatic portrayal of the unlimited possibilities for current and future generations of exiles: a new beginning is possible. The

20 Brathwaite, *The Arrivants* 108.
21 Brathwaite, *The Arrivants* 13.

Omowale archetype, like his counterpart in *Labyrinths,* is a symbol of that beginning. A candid offering and declaration of his inner longings has the potential to bring about the Omowale's cleansing. With this sacrificial offering up of his sins he can begin to assume the ideal stance for worship:

> I will rise
> and stand on my feet
>
> slowly slowly
> ever so slowly
>
> I will rise
> and stand on my feet
>
> like *akoko* the cock
> like *akoko* the cock
>
> who cries
> who cries in the morning
>
> *akoko bon'opa*
> *akoko tua bon*
>
> I am learning
> let me succeed
>
> I am learning
> let me succeed.[22]

Both the Omowale and Okigbo's initiate therefore share a similar experience, which has its origins in a culturopolitical process, and each reacts with a similar initial reluctance and inward trepidation. It is the infiltration by external forces of the body politic, the body social, and, fundamentally, the body spiritual which has given rise to the need for renewed processes of initiation. Imperialism, conquest, colonialism, and individual greed have made sure that the children of contemporary west African and West Indian societies can no longer look their God in the eye without a sense of guilt or betrayal. Their trans-

22 Brathwaite, *The Arrivants* 156.

formed setting and situations always seem to place them in direct antithesis to their superior being, whose response never seems to readily come when the imperfect subject nervously asks: 'Lord, is it I?'.

Okigbo's 'Limits' is all about self-realization and mortification. It is in 'Limits' that the initiate's first true confession takes place; and though the cost of confession is great, this is the beginning of a critical process. In Brathwaite's 'Limits' (*Masks*) mortification is pretty much the theme as well, where a type of death follows the claustrophobic groping of a people in 'The Forest'; but this appears an essential for a second birth. Here in *Masks* it is not the sunbird per se, but one nonetheless sees the symbolic reformation of life:

> From the womb'd heaven comes the new curled god
> with goblin old man's grinning, flat face smiling
> crouched like a frog with monkey hands and
> insect fingers.[23]

This is the birth of a new god, Ananse. He takes on the deformed look of his birthplace, but such is the price which spiritual delinquency seems to engender, in the same way that Okigbo's initiate's prodigality had left him with the 'scar of the crucifix'. Okigbo and Brathwaite are therefore seen to be very much concerned with the gateway between life, death, and rebirth, and both operate somewhere within that nebulous world of the half-dream which Okigbo speaks about. For Brathwaite this concern is not a stylistic end in itself: he is merely attempting to convey the magical realism of the setting and subject matter that he treats. Readers and critics who have drawn attention to and criticized his fantastical experiments in *Masks* have therefore misunderstood his prime objective. His method here is to signal the sense of ceremony, grandeur, and tragedy that imbues the history of African-Caribbean society. He would

23 Brathwaite, *The Arrivants* 116.

have been less effective had he not attempted such a powerful yet candid portrait in *Masks*. He needed to capture the setting – its nuances, sounds, traditions, beliefs, and rhythms. All of these were essential to embellish that philosophy of spiritual death and renewalwhich has for a long time fired his creative imagination.

The public voices so audibly presented and sounded in *Masks* seem a direct contrast to the relatively private ones in 'Heavensgate' and 'Limits'. Both poets have still attracted criticism: Beier and his school have taken Okigbo to task for excessive obscurity, whilst Brathwaite's presentation has been called lofty and flamboyant by critics like Ho Lung.

Although both poets have begun with an innate dilemma, it is significant that their treatments could throw up such contrasts of form and style. One way of approaching their difference is by route of their biographies (presented earlier in this book): a closer scrutiny of their respective quandaries and distinctive disciplinary bias can account for some of the differences perceived. What is quite clear about Brathwaite's own experiences before his personal encounter with west Africa is that he had left his native land, had travelled to Cambridge, the eponymous seat of academia in many British (not to mention West Indian) minds, and was there active amongst a growing body of creative thinkers and writers until, as he puts it: 'West Africa had given me a sense of place of belonging, and that place and belonging, I knew was the West Indies'.[24] So his initiation began.

His was the experience of an Omowale, one who could not hear the drum. Here was a type of intellectual poverty, a sterility that became even more self-evident when he found himself in Ghana, the land of his ancestors. As a historian coming into contact with a lifestyle that he knew must have

24 Rosalie Murphy, *Contemporary Poets of the English Language* (London: St James Press Ltd., 1970) 127.

been his own in the past, he needed to give fuller expression to the leavening forces of his ancestral past. Like the protagonist of the poem 'Francina', whose manner of dealing with the past had caused the narrow, politically focused observers to question what she wanted with a 'wrinkle face monster' of time, Brathwaite's preoccupation with the deeper cultural and spiritual meaning of the past has drawn criticism. As a historian it is not surprising that he reached for a holistic, historically slanted approach in *Masks*. But as a creative artist it is instructive that his treatment of the material is not linear, hard-set history. His work is therefore an admixture of personal encounter and historical fact, which contributes to the effectiveness of the structure and lends to the powerful grandeur of his first trilogy *The Arrivants*. Elsewhere[25] I have dealt with the distinction between art and pure history in Brathwaite's *The Arrivants*. It is Gordon Rohlehr who notes what he considers 'the first interesting point about Brathwaite's treatment of history in *Masks*', when he remarks that the seven kingdoms of the prelude to 'Libation' 'are not named in chronological order';[26] indeed, a similar signal had been thrown up as early as *Rights of Passage*, which reconfirms the suspicions that Brathwaite's sensibility has for a long time been shaped by his philosophy. The many lapses in time sequence and the rapid spatial movements across the continents in *Rights of Passage* re-emphasize Brathwaite's commitment to thematic development at the expense of chronology. Then, too, his style reveals a preoccupation with the psyche, a feature which takes him to much analytical depth and which like the korabra, the funeral drum, goes to the roots of experience and returns again. All in all his is a vision which one might refer to as being three-dimensional, with linear/chronological, spatial/thematic, and abstruse/analytical parameters.

25 In a Caribbean Studies Thesis on 'Time, Ritual and Rebirth in *The Arrivants*'. (U.W.I: Cave Hill Campus, 1988) 3–6.

26 Gordon Rohlehr, *Pathfinder* (Tunapuna: Gordon Rohlehr, 1981) 118.

Clearly, Okigbo did not set out to reach for and recreate the many institutions that define his race and its history. He preferred to offer his treatment of the Igbo's plight symbolically, through the dealings of his own self – personal to some extent, but ultimately no less vivid than a more public approach might engender. A leaning towards the classics, with their reliance on the allegory and symbolism, was an important contributor to Okigbo's form, method, and style in treating his theme. But he also drew very heavily on local and indigenous influences as he sought to make sense of his and his people's struggle in Igboland and Nigeria.

If Brathwaite's prodigal in *Masks* suffers from spiritual amnesia, then the initiate of 'Heavensgate' appears to be harbouring a spiritual guilt brought on by infidelity to his indigenous beliefs. But both have sensed the extent of their estrangement from a tradition, and they full well know what is responsible: hence their separate undertakings.

CHAPTER 8

X/Self and the Second Trilogy: Harmony and Departures

Kamau Brathwaite is without doubt one of the most provocative, complex, yet rewarding of world poets. His work has attracted considerable attention outside but also within its native region, especially with respect to its stylistic conventions and esoteric experiments. This was the case with the first trilogy, and remains so today.[1] If the first trilogy *The Arrivants* (*Rights of Passage, Masks, Islands*) marked the etching out of his discursive and stylistic method, then the second trilogy (*Mother Poem, Sun Poem, X/Self*) was even more pivotally placed in establishing his method, focus, and ideological pathway.

To some extent the second trilogy's final instalment (*X/Self*) was a key moment for this poet, whose work was clearly evolving into a systematic ripple of outward yet inward movements, like the tides on the shore of the islands that gave impetus to his creative spirit. In hindsight, *X/Self* is clearly not his most ambitious or abstruse project; but if placed in the context of the second trilogy, then it certainly is. It is within this parameter that this chapter seeks to examine *X/Self*. If it is read within the parameters of the first and second trilogies, how does *X/Self* fit in? How does it interface with, how does it relate

1 See a reading of Brathwaite's first trilogy in Gordon Rohlehr, *Pathfinder* (Tunapuna: Gordon Rohlehr, 1981). See Emily Allen Williams, *The Critical Response to Kamau Brathwaite* (Westport: Greenwood, 2004). See Curwen Best's reading of Brathwaite within a conceptualization of Barbadian aesthetics in chs 1 and 2 of *Roots to Popular Culture* (London: Macmillan, 2001) 4–89.

to Brathwaite's main stream of work at the time? This chapter will consider *X/Self*'s compatibility/harmony with/in the second trilogy; it also wants to consider the nature of its dissonance. It does so by conducting a close reading of theme, content, and stylistic features. In the same way that Okigbo's 'Path of Thunder' is often discussed in terms of its compatibility within the *Labyrinths* collection, *X/Self*'s place in the second trilogy is also disputed.

In the final analysis, an understanding of *X/Self*'s dynamics can provide critical insight into what Torres-Saillant calls Brathwaite's 'daring succession of imaginative leaps'.[2] As a result we better appreciate the kinds of stylistic, conceptual, and methodological shifts that the poet negotiates from time to time, or stumbles upon in the immediacy of constructing concentric ripples across his 'tidalectic' enterprise. Brathwaite has developed the concept of tidalectics to help explain the ongoing dynamic, fluid relationship between competing epistemologies. He is especially concerned with Caribbean society and the struggle for control of the region, hence the use of the ocean/sea/tide metaphor; but he is also concerned with global dynamics, and dialectics. His work is therefore regional and international in focus.

There have been several articles and books that have analysed *X/Self*. Some within this number have tended to focus on *X/Self*'s struggle with itself over the years since its publication. They have addressed the issue of its several versions, for instance comparing the original 1987 version with the 2001 version which appeared in *Ancestors*, the name given to the second trilogy.[3] Others have discussed the creative excesses of

2 Silvio Torres-Saillant, 'The Trials of Authenticity in Kamau Brathwaite' in *World Literature Today*, 68, (1994).

3 See Kelly Baker Josephs, 'Versions of *X/Self*: Kamau Brathwaite's Caribbean Discourse'. *Anthurium*, 1, 1 Fall, (2003). <http://scholar.library.miami.edu/anthurium/volume_1/issue_1/josephs-versions.htm>. Accessed July 30, 2007.

the work itself: for instance, Joyelle McSweeney comments about its 'rollicking trans-global, anachronistic series of poems'.[4]

The focus on the several versions is a worthwhile undertaking, especially in light of the fact that the publication of *Ancestors* reveals what might very well be considered a second edition of the collection called *X/Self*. But not enough studies have focused on the original publication, giving full weight to the fact that this was the poem's first 'complete' delivery in print. An examination of the work in the context of the time of its first delivery arguably enables a keener discussion of the work's location in the second trilogy, where it was given conceptual flesh and presented to the reading public. This is a necessary project, especially if, as I do, one considers Brathwaite's two trilogies as products of the Independence era. Like Okigbo's work these two collections owe their existence to the sociocultural and political climate of the late 1950s and 1960s. Okigbo's *Labyrinths* reflects the actual intellectual milieu of the Independence period. The entire poem therefore displays a tension between a range of competing epistemologies, beliefs, conditions, ambitions, and desires. Its themes and issues are personal and private, but also public and poignantly real. While Okigbo was cut off way too soon, his poetry has in a strange way remained poignantly present, hovering around his society and wider nation as they struggled to gain regional and international status, long after the Independence era gave way to the global mindset. Like Okigbo's *Labyrinths*, Brathwaite's two trilogies contain the issues and aspirations of that period. They are both ambitious ventures, constituting radical interventions into their respective cultural and political spaces. Although *X/Self* appeared in the 1980s, its association with the two previous collections helps to mark it as Brathwaite's greatest achievement of the Independence era, and partly for this reason it is

4 Joyelle McSweeney, 'Kamau Brathwaite, *Ancestors*'. *Octopus Magazine* Issue 5. (2001). <http://www.octopusmagazine.com/issue05/recovery_project/mcsweeney_on_brathwaite.htm>. Accessed July 30, 2007.

necessary to read and assess *X/Self* within such a context. This chapter therefore performs that kind of enquiry: it is less concerned with the fact of the revision of the poems, but pays more attention to reading the original collection in its moment. If we accept that Brathwaite's two trilogies define his major work of the Independence period, what is his 'final' vision offered within that period? If 'Path of Thunder' is Okigbo's parting song, *X/Self* can be considered Brathwaite's summation within that period. What does it say? If Okigbo is transformed from artist/priest to town crier by the end of his career, what is the nature of Brathwaite's transformation?

1. Prelude

The fear and reservation which Kamau Brathwaite expresses at the outset of *X/Self* about his copious notes to the text/poetry is indicative of the dilemma which looms over the artist who is writing for two kinds of audience, the one academic and the other folk: 'The poetry of *X/Self* is based on a culture that is personal-i-man/caribbean – and multifarious, with the learning and education that this implies.'[5] Almost apologetically he beckons:

> So the notes ... which I hope are helpful, but which I provide with great reluctance, since the irony is that they may suggest the poetry is so obscure in itself that it has to be lighted up; is so lame, that it has to have a crutch; and (most hurtful of all) that it is bookish, academic, 'history'.[6]

And in some respects sounding like the enigmatic Christopher Okigbo, who had partly attributed his poetry's perceived ob-

5 Edward Brathwaite, *X/Self* (Oxford: Oxford University Press, 1987) 113.
6 Brathwaite, *X/Self* 113.

scurity to a deficiency in his most immediate audience, Brathwaite explains:

> Because Caribbean culture has been so cruelly neglected both by the Caribbean itself and by the rest of the world (except for spot/check and catch-ups via cricket and reggae), my references (my nommos and icons) may appear mysterious, meaningless even, to both Caribbean and non-Caribbean readers.[7]

What has made the experience of producing *X/Self* that bit more painful for Brathwaite is his stated objective of speaking about and to the folk, through folk forms. In the collections that precede *X/Self* – *Mother Poem* and *Sun Poem* – Brathwaite is at home, and in more ways than one. Conversely in *X/Self* he wrestles to convince the reader that he and they are both at home.[8] They are, if they are willing to undergo a process of magical proportions. If Okigbo's *Labyrinths* is marked by the poet's embracing of indigenous motifs, then Brathwaite's second trilogy seems to present an opposite movement towards the proliferation of universal motifs.

From *Mother Poem*'s second poem 'Twine' to its anti-penultimate 'Peace Fire' the local voice with its 'nation language' is that cadence most potently sounded, giving way occasionally to the more formal-sounding authorial voice which is first heard in 'Alpha'. These two voices are observed in 'Twine', which offers to engage the reader in conversation:

> My husband
> if you cud see he
> fragile, fraid o'e own shadow
> he does let de man boss e' bout in de job
> like e got a dog in de corner.[9]

7 Brathwaite, *X/Self* 113.
8 Brathwaite, *X/Self* 113.
9 Edward Brathwaite, *Mother Poem* (Oxford: Oxford University Press, 1977) 6.

and in 'Alpha', whose tone is more impersonal and almost devoid of emotion:

> The ancient watercourses of my island
> echo of river, trickle, worn stone,
> the sunken voice of glitter inching its pattern to the sea,
> memory of foam, fosil, erased beaches high above the eaten
> boulders of st. philip
> my mother is a pool ...[10]

But the authorial voice can also become actively involved and intimate, perhaps under pressure, as the woman has to 'venture out into the mercantile shame/rock' within part II ('Nightwash') in the poem 'Woo/Dove':

> so what she go do
> three years now she was tekkin
> commercial down at de modern, mekkin
>
> shorthan' while she learning to type
> but she dear-aunt done dead
> de one who did payin de school
> fees ...[11]

A similar interplay of voices is also evident within *Sun Poem*. Commencing with the resolute authorial voice like that which ended off *Mother Poem, Sun Poem* soon gives over to a preponderance of 'nation language' usage by the speaking voices and by the named characters on reaching part III ('Son') No. 8, 'of all the boys on the beach':

> but your parents were vague if
> you asked where it was what it meant you were told
> place where the bad boys went
>
> ii
>
> when when he was he didn't know how much then, batto had burss

10 Brathwaite, *Mother Poem* 3.
11 Brathwaite, *Mother Poem* 42–43.

another boy eye in a fight
it was so:

you does stann toe to toe knee to knee and does stare at each
udder wid a fowlcock eye

then one is step back an tro dung e cap an comman
touch dat ...[12]

X/Self does not reflect the level of stylistic interplay found within *Mother Poem* and *Sun Poem*. In *X/Self* their linguistic range is stated but not explored. Caribbean 'nation language' is not the major mode of communication for the poetry within *X/Self*, as it was in *Sun Poem*.

This is but one of the telling distinctions between this text and the rest of the second trilogy (and especially telling in light of Brathwaite's cultural-linguistic outlook). Firstly this might give rise to speculations about the organic wholeness of the second trilogy; secondly it brings to the fore the question of Brathwaite's style: whether *X/Self* marks a moment of stylistic transformation or signals a conscious development on the part of the artist; or maybe *X/Self* is not substantially new if a careful analysis of it is undertaken.

2. Harmony of the Second Trilogy

Anthony Kellman considers *X/Self* a 'staggering lyrical fusion of European, Amerindian, African and Maroon landscapes that reassesses Caribbean Man in all his playfulness, complexity and pathos': but he reads it as a 'continuation of the journey

12 Edward Brathwaite, *Sun Poem* (Oxford: Oxford University Press, 1982) 15–16.

Brathwaite articulated in *Rights of Passage*'.[13] In support of the outlook conveyed in Kellman's review of *X/Self* it must be said that there are general similarities between the texts which make up the second trilogy. These parallels exist particularly at the level of theme, structure (textual and verbal), and notably with respect to experimentation with words/sounds/song-play.

Mother Poem and *Sun Poem* take up the themes of dislocation, exploitation, and the movement towards affirmation (concerns which had previously formed the centrepiece of *The Arrivants*), and they deal with them within the parameters and peculiarity of a specific island setting. The Mother's precarious existence results as much from the ignominies of the past, as from the perpetuation and re-institutionalization of the values that slavery fostered. The poem 'Miss Own', with its almost humiliating and repetitive 'sign a bill here', re-emphasizes the continuation of the Mother's condition of inferiority, and dependency: since the woman is presumed to be both illiterate and untrustworthy the task is not hers to sign the bills; the merchant does not allow it, she must 'stick' to the shoes; that is the sum of their relationship:

> for the shoe is a safe cottage to the illiterate peasant
> needing light/ running water, the indestructible plastic of the soft
> ill
> lit/erate present
>
> *sign a bill here*[14]

Sun Poem also reveals a lingering concern with the complexities brought on by a history of slavery. The development of the boy Adam is mirrored by the parallel recounting of the development of the island. This relationship goes beyond the pathetic

13 Anthony Kellman, 'A Rich Plural Heritage as a Tool for Survival', A review of *X/Self* by Edward Kamau Brathwaite. *Callaloo,* 36 (Summer, 1988): 645–648.

14 Brathwaite, *Mother Poem* 36–37.

fallacy. Each is made to seem to depend on the other for fuller conceptualization, and Brathwaite achieves this by juxtaposing scenes of his character's development with those of the island. The nerve-racking 'hearse hill' experience, for instance, is juxtaposed with the account of an equally precarious period in West Indian history, that of slavery. In section V ('The Crossing') the cliff-hanging journey begins:

> up... up... up...
> the engines droned up ...
>
> trees leaning closer
> and closer and closer across the sides of the road ...
>
> watching the hemmed-in boys in the buses
> whispering... watching... watching and watching ...
>
> *hearse hill*
>
> everyone quiet/no clapping no/gladsong
> only the sad sad song of the doomed and clambering bus ...[15]

and immediately following, in section VI ('Noom'), the entrapped slave begs for respite: 'remember us now in this sweat juiced jail in / this hail of cutlass splinters of cane in this / pale sail to soil'.[16] And just as Adam is prepared to take on 'a new world opening up inside', so too the islands are giving birth to those (like the Barbadian national hero Bussa), who are equally willing to be free from the confines of 'dis meat box',

> an de white
> people vex
>
> let we fight
> in instead a flight
>
> in from dem jess be
> cause a dis man

15 Brathwaite, *Sun Poem* 43.
16 Brathwaite, *Sun Poem* 53.

who couldn't care less
bout defeat: what name so:

e mane bussa[17]

Other associated themes, such as a concern with spirituality, are explored within *Sun Poem* and *Mother Poem* as well. Poems such as 'Sam Lord', 'Bell', and 'Prayer' in *Mother Poem* are concerned with the corruption that infects much of institutionalized religion. *Sun Poem* is less to do with religion as a system, but it presents elements of religion, which inform and underscore the progression of the work.

X/Self is equally concerned with alienation, exploitation, and religious misrepresentation. The Mother's plight, which weighed so heavily in the preceding books of the second trilogy, returns with equal foreboding in *X/Self*. In the poem 'Donna' the setting is no longer Barbadian, but the situation is the same. The female expresses her fear of society's violation, of 'the girl raped in her own house', itself a violent reality which foreshadows another type of violence, the forced self-infliction that is witnessed in 'Twoom'; there, set against 'the present hunger on the pavement' there is 'the mother of five pickney I will drop to red gal ring / to/morrow night' in Jamaica.[18]

This is what the female must resort to in order to survive. In 'Donna' the inevitability of a life of prostitution had been expressed by the female speaking voice:

an de man want i sleep wid im
an me got me exam

an de man seh mek i go wid im
an me can barely bear to look pan im

17 Brathwaite, *Sun Poem* 60.
18 Brathwaite, *X/Self* 90.

> *but wha ya guh do when yu belly gone slack an yu young gifted*
> *an na idiot ...*[19]

Like her counterparts in *Mother Poem* and *Sun Poem*, she is well aware of 'dese man who is here tonight an tomorrow dem ganne', but at the present there seems to be no easy escape, for even when she chooses to be independent of men a type of disillusionment and ennui invariably sets in as well.

'X/Self's Xth Letters from The Thirteen Provinces' is a testament to the ongoing process of false security which a formal education had engendered in *Mother Poem*. Chalkstick, the teacher of 'Lix' and 'Occidente', harbours other ambitions besides those over which he has reassured the mother about her son 'that the boy would be a *lux occidentc*'. For after he listens to her he smiles, 'accepting another black hostage of verbs'.[20] The character X/Self is the regimented, unthinking product of Chalkstick's ambitions. In his letter written abroad from the Thirteen Provinces to his mother he is at the mercy of computer/education tool, machine, master, planter, firstly expressing his elation at 'learning prospero linguage' and then confessing his gut-felt doubts about his whole experience:

> a fine
> a cyaan get nutten
>
> write
>
> a cyaan get nutten really
> rite
> while a stannin up here in me years like I inside a me shadow ...
>
> yet a sittin down here in front a dis stone
> face/ eeee
>
> lectrical mallet into me
> fist

19 Brathwaite, *X/Self* 71–72.
20 Brathwaite, *Mother Poem* 24.

chipp/in dis poem onta dis tablet
chiss/ellin darkness writin in light

like i is a some/is a some/is a some
body/a

x

pert or some
thing like moses or aaron or one a dem dyaam isra
lite

&
mam

why is
dat?

what it
mean?[21]

He cannot quite understand the sense of loss that afflicts his soul. His education has taught him to know the computer (hardware), but he is not able to supply the necessary input/ data; hence a sense of alienation results.

The exploitation of the colonized and neocolonized is continued throughout *X/Self* as well. The injustices presented in *Sun Poem*'s 'Noom' are given fuller development in *X/Self*'s 'Nuum', which recalls a period of cultural and spiritual innocence ('green pastures'), and the subsequent conquests by 'the miners of the empire', who play upon the general affable nature of the original dwellers but then 'they destroy they / destroy they destroy they do not care'.[22]

'Shaman', 'Edge of the desert', 'X/plosive video tape salesman', and 'The visibility trigger' all take up this theme, while the latter is especially forceful in its presentation. The contrasting image of 'kola nut' (a symbol of greeting) and 'gunfire' is as shocking as the hellfire that actually lands upon the 'unreal

21 Brathwaite, *X/Self* 85–87.
22 Brathwaite, *X/Self* 35.

virginal elders' in 'The visibility trigger'. This is but one example from what is perhaps the most disturbingly potent of all the poems in *X/Self*. It is infested with visual, aural, and olfactory images of perfidy and violence:

i offered you a kola nut
your fingers huge and smooth and red
and you took it your dress makola blue

and you broke it into gunfire

the metal was hot and jagged
it was as if the master of bronze

had poured anger into his cauldron

and let it spit spit sputter
and it was black spark green in my face ...[23]

The clash of human flesh with inorganic and metallic implements is especially chilling.

In *X/Self* the Church and State function in tandem as enforcers of rule. In the poem 'The fapal state machine' the letter of the law, and all sense as well, is lost in a conglomeration/muddle of legal/judicial and sacerdotal dogma:

2

above all
sense of order

consider law
itself and for

itself itself

and then the precepts
that are crooked within

itself itself

23 Brathwaite, *X/Self* 48.

> say whether they be good or bad and if they come from god
> and if from god whether from god from god or througn an
>
> agency like angles or from some other agency or does it come
> from god at all ...[24]

Quite symbolically as well, the 'new man' in the poem 'And now a soft commentaries from Angelo Solimann Africanus the Neumann' is 'priest or politician', and he makes no secret of his unbroken allegiance: 'for the church / for the state for the state machine / for the merchant banker ...'.

Word-sound and song-play is still a noticeable feature of Brathwaite's style up into *X/Self*. 'X/plosive videotape salesman' is representative of the poet's attitude in his most satirical, cunning and biting delivery. It portrays the conversation between the salesman, a 'nobel peace plize winner' who has 'just invented plunder', and a prospective customer/victim. It readily lends itself to dramatic interpretation and performance (portraying a telephone conversation), and in this respect it comes quite close to a form on which *Sun Poem* has thrived. This poem 'X/plosive videotape salesman' makes use of the jagged line, employing broken words and/or phrases to potent effect, often to convey some hidden meaning. For example, the deliberate splitting of 'nobel' into 'no / bel', calls to mind the French word 'bel', which means 'beautiful' or perhaps 'good', suggesting 'no good'. Hence, the X/posive videotape saleman's 'hello' and introduction becomes more revelatory than it initially appears:

> Hello
> Hello
> Hello
> hello

24 Brathwaite, *X/Self* 18–19.

i
am the no

bel peace plize winner ...[25]

This is the extent to which the artist's manipulation of verse can take him. Quite often Brathwaite's method has the effect of startling the reader, firstly through his pertinent and vivid sound/word echoes, and secondly through his cunning experimentation with rhythm. For example, the representation of 'saying' as 'shaying' in the question: 'you can't understand what I / shaying?' not only introduces the notion of incomprehension between salesman and customer, but it manifests their type of misunderstanding as being one with language; it is with this very language and words that the poet creates tension, as in the two-metre, four-bar phrase which begins this poem, and which is repeated throughout ('hello/hello/hello/hello ...'), remaining unresolved at the end of the poem:

hell/o
hell/o
hell/o
hell/ [26]

Its faltering syllabic rhythm echoes the unwholesomeness of the salesman's designs, and the final lexical item ('hell') blows an ill wind that underscores the approximate threat of destruction.

The allusion to the music and the musicians of the 'new world' continues to form the frame of reference for which Brathwaite is well known. In 'Shaman' the 'coming together' (in principle) of Black and White on the plantation is depicted with the imagery of ebony and ivory. And Brathwaite makes it known that the inspiration for this imagery is derived from the pop song 'Ebony and Ivory' by Stevie Wonder and Paul

25 Brathwaite, *X/Self* 40.
26 Brathwaite, *X/Self* 47.

McCartney, with its pretentious ('glamourous') portrayal of harmony. The reality of this fragile relationship between Black and White is echoed in the reference to Bob Marley's 'Get up Stand up', where the colonized confesses 'i just can't get / up stand / up stand / up for i rights.'[27]

But the rhythm of Shango which is present in many African diasporic rhythms and styles, including Marley's reggae, persists throughout times of suppression (as in 'Shaman'); and ultimately the god of thunder who had possessed *Mother Poem*'s 'Angel/Engine' places his stamp upon the 'new world' within *X/Self*:

> after so many twists
> after so many journeys
> after so many changes
>
> bop hard bop soul bop funk
> new thing marley soul rock skank
> *bunk Johnson is riding again ...*
>
> your thunder has come home.[28]

3. *X/Self* Departures

X/Self's grand universal frame of reference situates it in sharp contrast to the local setting and situations that hitherto formed the core of Brathwaite's second trilogy. *Mother Poem*'s inspiration comes from an aesthetic response to the poet's islandscape, and it becomes a literary testament to the vitality of the island's flora and fauna, its language and its people. Such a preoccupation is also the pledge of *Sun Poem*, whose appearance in 1982 signalled that the second trilogy would be the

27 Brathwaite, *X/Self* 67.
28 Brathwaite, *X/Self* 110–111.

artist's dedicated tribute to the land of his birth, Barbados. But *X/Self* takes one beyond the boundaries of the island and the archipelago, and seeks to submerge one's sensibility within a culture that is (yes, both 'personal' and 'Caribbean', but) saliently universal.

If *Sun* and *Mother* poems emanate from the personal relationship with an island, *X/Self*'s inspiration and unifying thread of thought seems to be the belief that there is such a thing as a universal culture of the deprived. *X/Self* is therefore an exercise in discovering the undiscovered; or, rather, the undisclosed. Its predominant icons are Black (African), Brown (creole), and Alexandrian figures, whose notable exploits often deny them the privilege of being perceived within their true racial context. The panoramic and historical overview of some of history's significant events supplied by 'Salt' incorporates the better-known figures such as 'L'Ouverture', 'che', and 'nancy' (anancy), but offers to educate and enlighten with regard the race and exploits of such as 'mohammet', 'socrates', 'moses', 'herod', and 'tutankhammen' as well.

Brathwaite is acutely aware that he has a task on his hands in delivering *X/Self* to his readership. Without appearing to be pedantic he has attempted to carry out his teaching by offering clues of association. For example, he places 'che', 'kismet', 'doctor castro', and 'ho chi minh' together, where to be familiar with one is to know what the others are: Third World liberators. And for reassurance he often discloses their association either within the context of the verse or in an accompanying statement; this is done for the lawgivers 'aaron hammurabi dracon' (although it should be said that his poetry per se offers less than a lucid education and places much onus on the reader, who must either be cognizant of one component of the clue, or be astute enough to garner sufficient information from the poem's contents and the clue's context.

Here one might consider the way the poet has attempted to disclose the relevance and relationship of the trio above. The word 'laws' is mentioned near to them, but so are 'glitter' and 'guilt'; so that if one is supposed to assume that these men are lawgivers then one might well have assumed that they are also guilt-ridden men:

> The sky has been cut into square blue holes in the ruined colosseum
> and there are no laws left no glitter no guilt
> aaron hammurabi dracon ... [29]

This stream of associations is attempted throughout *X/Self*. For example, there is 'cong', 'john brown', and 'jack johnson', all 'third world rebels', in 'Nix'; 'Equiano', 'paul / robeson', and 'othello the moor', all distinguished men who are contrasted to the heinous 'black faces' of exploitation which 'come out of the ground' in 'Nuum'. The same also occurs with names of historical places and events. Through this method Brathwaite is attempting a compromise between neither being overtly authoritarian in his versenor too esoteric: but he often ends up being both. The clues that he offers within the poetry itself are often not enough for the reader (academics included), and his endnotes inflict a heavy burden on those readers who will turn to them to find their way through his labyrinthine frame of reference within *X/Self*. The native readers of *Sun* and *Mother* poems must find the experience of reading the poetry in *X/Self* much more taxing, and as demanding as the formal educational process which is needed in order to gain a substantive command of European and Caribbean history.

The familiar Brown's Beach and Pie Corner are replaced by settings as diverse as Aachen and Texcoco Tenochtitlan and the native adam and his symbolic mother give way to Charlemagne and Hannibal in *X/Self*. Although this is only a simplification of the dynamic transformations that are taking place within the collection, it begins to offer reasons for *X/Self*'s uniqueness. The

29 Brathwaite, *X/Self* 6.

panoramic outlook of *X/Self* has resulted in an episodic-type presentation and a showcasing of many characters, so that there is no 'real' character development of the extent achieved in the previous books of poetry.

It can be argued that X/Self is the leading personality in *X/Self*, as adam, the mother and the father were in the previous collections, but his character does not achieve the type of attention, insight, or development which was accorded the former icons. These former icons are the central components to their individual books of poetry, and the preoccupation with developing their characters is to a great extent responsible for the folk-oriented texture that their poems possess. That preoccupation has resulted in the portrayal of their lifestyles, their location, and, quite noticeably, their language. *X/Self* does not show the same commitment to characterization, neither in terms of local identity nor in terms of character development. In *X/Self* one is only given vignettes of the folksy reality that possessed *Mother* and *Sun* poems. The nation-language variety which makes up the latter half of 'Donna' is reminiscent of that of *Mother Poem* both in terms of style (the basilectal variety) and content (hardships), but it is quite rare in *X/Self*:

an lard how it hot how a greasy
and de pickney dress dem fe done

an de lang track a night tick tickin tick tickin
machine petal shattering on
an de clock stuck at 1.35 1.55 1.35 1.55

see how me yeye cyaan prop open even
an de rent fe pay
an anoder one comin tomarrow ...[30]

'X/Self's Xth Letters from the Thirteen Provinces' displays a similar stylistic inclination. However, one feels that characters like 'X/Self' and 'Donna' are mere constructs for a greater

30 Brathwaite, *X/Self* 71.

design, since they themselves and the language variety which they speak are soon replaced by an array of world figures and by a poetic tone that almost always holds fast to an approximate standard variety. The beginning of 'Ice/Nya' is quite characteristic of this major mode of communication within *X/Self*:

> And so the greeks return and are recognized
> and so are the ithacans and the battlements of troy
>
> virgil invents aeneas as they set out for civilization
> with wounds nourished in the bloodstreams of angst
>
> pyramids come down to the rivers to drink
> ankh osiris isis
>
> and you make of me mysteries foundationless histories ...[31]

There is no consistent, pervasive folk voice with which the reader readily identifies and through whom his/her perspective is constantly filtered. After going with such an accompaniment throughout *Mother Poem* and *Sun Poem,* the native reader finds *X/Self*'s dominant poetic voice to be different. It is on occasion accessible, but it often transcends local and regional boundaries, opting for a larger frame of reference. The poem 'Phalos' is a characteristic example in this regard. Here one can observe the interplay between the folk-oriented reference ('buttock down, cooking pot, eddoes eschak') and its converse ('camelot, yehudi'), as the poet remarks about the types of transformations that have taken hold on 'our women':

> and now they cannot buttock down to hearth or cooking pot
> to tumtum achar eddoes
>
> they dream of rubenstein of vogue and guinevere at camelot
> at arthurs fogey castle

31 Brathwaite, *X/Self* 102.

they have become wise foolish virgins credit card viragoes
yehudi burns them into violins of sacramental fire

like eschak mescak and abednegro ...[32]

In the poem 'Nix' Caesar appears as 'Richard Nix'; in 'Salt' Julia, Caesar's 'daughter, is pompey's wife', and subsequently in 'Julia' she reappears as 'caesars young mulatto sister'. Brathwaite refers to these apparent incongruities as part of his 'magical realism'. This is a device with which he comes to experiment quite freely throughout *X/Self*; in fact, his notes refer quite liberally to the occurrences of this stylistic phenomenon. There are few other occurrences of bona fide magical realism within the second trilogy outside *X/Self*. This is not to say that magical realism is completely new to Brathwaite's poetry, for certainly Ogun the Yoruban creative/destructive god of thunder metamorphosed into the poet's uncle in the magical realism of the poem 'Ogun' in the book of poetry called *Islands*. But the density of its occurrence in *X/Self* makes the work stand out from the others in the second trilogy. The type and degree of surrealism within *X/Self* makes it reminiscent of the style associated with such South American writers as Gabriel García Márquez. Magical realism, morbid decay and corruption, and senseless violence, are three of the notable features of that movement, and these are manifested in the work *X/Self*.

For Márquez, Macondo is a village that exists at the edge of reality. There time stops,[33] and all else takes over: corruption, greed, all forms of decay[34] (spiritual, political, mental, etc.); and when the sun ultimately sets it is only a signal that the cycle will be repeated. The world portrayed in *X/Self* certainly is not as deeply pessimistic, but its unrelenting and potent portrayal of spiritual, political, and mental decay makes it quite similar, at the least.

32 Brathwaite, *X/Self* 16.

33 Gabriel García Márquez, *In Evil Hour* (London: Jonathan Cape, 1979) 125.

34 Márquez, *In Evil Hour* 7 and 8.

Spiritual and political corruption have for the most part already been touched upon within a thematic framework, but here it is useful to compare the intensity with which it is presented within *X/Self,* as against the *Mother Poem* presentation. 'Peace Fire' (*Mother Poem*) examines the pernicious effects of selfish self-rule, an idea also taken up in *X/Self*'s 'The fapal state machine'.

The portent of doom and destruction described in 'Peace Fire' is climaxed with the image of 'Babylon the Great Mother of Harlocks And Abominations',[35] undoubtedly an ill omen. However, 'The fapal state machine' not only foretells the type of calamity that looms, but it gives a vivid portrayal of the actual apocalypse. The State machine is said to be created to combat all of the evils of the past, but instead the violent irony of the poem is that it (the machine) will oversee the re-enactment of those very evils:

> there will be
> cinemas of buchenwald lit with sarcophagi of gas
>
> there will be
> laden vessels in the night ablaze with spice and jewels
>
> on an iceberg
>
> there will be
> armies bleeding in their bivouacks and living off the rattas
>
> of the land
>
> there will be
> changeling priests to chant you pop instead of litany
>
> there will be
> would be healers festering like mangoes at the bottom of the bag …
>
> there will be
> scabbard legions clashing in the night

35 Brathwaite, *Mother Poem* 107.

there will be
riots fires insurrections nkrumah's heedless statue broken down

the universal sun eclipsed by man and time and chaos ...[36]

'a soft commentaries' is built around the violence, putridity, and decay of human life, which surpasses even that seen in 'The fapal state machine'. The skulls of the decapitated (Aztecs, Congolese), are the foundation, the material with which the 'white blazing pyramids' (more lofty than those of Egypt) are made: Brathwaite represents the horror of the violation and its innumerable casualties through the following:[37]

00500
0005000
000050000
00000500000
0000005000000
000000050000000
00000000500000000
0000000005000000000
+0000000005000000000+

and it could go on for ever and ever and ever ...

What is most particularly reminiscent of Márquez (and some South American writing) is the treatment of the 'thick portly women' in 'Letter from Roma'. For Márquez physical description of a character is often a clue about the character's inner traits. The following scene from *La Mala Hora* is a forceful comment on the clergy, here symbolized by El Padre Angel (Father Angel):

> Tuesday, October fourth, he thought; and in a low voice he said: 'St. Francis of Assisi'. He got dressed without washing and without praying.

36 Brathwaite, *X/Self* 20–21.
37 Brathwaite, *X/Self* 57.

> He was large, ruddy, with the peaceful figure of a domesticated ox, and he moved like an ox, with thick, sad gestures.[38]

Father Angel's scant regard for the duties of his calling, dressing without washing and praying, seems an indictment of the priestly calling. His description as being like a domesticated ox says much more about this character's inner quality than anything else.

The emperor's son, the protagonist of the poem 'Letter from Roma', sinks into a trance where the scents in his room and the salacious sensuality of his encounter with the 'widow dowagers' fuse and lull his senses into a surreal experience quite similar to the many which pervade *La Mala Hora* (p. 10):

> already while I wait my head goes giddy
>
> their fat bejewelled fingers clammy hands
>
> that search me out: tieing a tassel: tapping a link
>
> make my blood itch: the mad blood fricates rise and rough
> me as they rub against the
> ridges of my vest
>
> and when they raise their arms
> the cologne waters of their last ablutions
> mingle with sticky wet and foetid vapours rising
>
> from their charms: I clutch ...[39]

These ladies' close association with the emperor and conqueror is an indirect comment on the leadership. The sight of 'greasy thighs' betrays their bearing, and ornate indignity. This is a stark and biting satire on leadership, also a notable stylistic feature and an important concern in Latin America literature.

In Brathwaite's magical realism (in the poem 'Mai Village') 'Six Men's', a Barbadian coastal fishing village, metamorphoses

38 Márquez, *In Evil Hour* 7.

39 Brathwaite, *X/Self* 3–4.

into 'my lai', the Vietnamese village 'where all the villagers were slaughtered' during the war of the late 1960s and early 1970s. For these villagers their sin is one of location. With little or no interest in politics they go about their day-to-day routines with nonchalance and ease, chewing 'gum sitting on the wall'. To have been born in such a village is to have been predestined to exist in a world over whose course one can have no control: here they are slaves to time, and to the circumstances of inequality and injustice in society, Brathwaite seems to say. The images are of 'rusting dwellings', 'grey' ancestors, and a general 'decay' which goes beyond anything seen in the *Sun* and *Mother* poems. It is people like the titan ('Titan') who are responsible for the destruction of such innocent lives; Mai lai and Tetemextltan are one and the same. In the poem the oppressor is Cortez, titan: and at the end he becomes transformed into the prince of darkness as well, when he confesses his misdeeds:

and so i overturned their idols rolled

them down the stairs and stare out at you from your
postage stamps

i
cortez condor clubfoot

evening star[40]

A work like *X/Self* cannot go unnoticed when it stands against other poems such as *Sun Poem* and *Mother Poem*. It is distinct from the other books of the second trilogy. Perhaps in retrospect one might say that it is no more conspicuous than *Masks* had been in the first trilogy. But whereas *Masks* reaffirms the Brathwaite philosophy, commitment, and style (expressed so clearly in *Rights of Passage* and *Islands*), *X/Self* seems to go beyond the domain of *Mother Poem* and *Sun Poem*. While this is a judgement made in relation to the second trilogy, one is not

40 Brathwaite, *X/Self* 63.

incredulous that Brathwaite could have written a collection like *X/Self*. For after all, he has gone on to produce other startling projects such as *Barabajan Poems* (1994) and *Golokwati* (2003). Given the poet's tendency towards experimental excursions, it has become customary to anticipate practical, conceptual, and intellectual challenges with the release of each new Brathwaite collection. The artist is always under constant pressure/compulsion to utter his voice. Brathwaite's inspiration in *X/Self* emanates from the need to further enlighten his readership with regards to the depth, magnitude, possibilities, and potency of the world's 'cultures of the deprived': 'Black', 'African', 'Latin', 'Asian'. An important lesson derived from *X/Self* and the second trilogy is that notions of harmony, dissonance, and intertextuality are relative. But this examination of the collection also points to the fact that contextualised/bracketed readings of the work are ever relevant.

Brathwaite's final work of the period is daring, ambitious, and liminal. It is like Okigbo's final offering in that regard. But Brathwaite's work here seems to look outward into a world that is not that familiar to many Caribbean people. In that regard he therefore courts the danger of alienating the very people for whom he writes. His vision of the region's future appears as refracted historical actions which gain renewed life in a globalized world. His vision presents Caribbean subjects as part of an even larger process of cultural, spiritual, and political decay. Some of his subjects therefore share an ambivalent attitude to the emerging era that promises to change the world for ever. The image of X/Self standing at the doorway of the technological age is especially vivid. The protagonist of Okigbo's later poetry does not stare this type of technology in the face, but is just as precariously poised at the gateway.

CHAPTER 9

Return of the Town Crier?: Okigbo's 'Path of Thunder' and *Labyrinths*

For the poet of 'Path of Thunder', unlike that of 'Heavensgate', 'Limits', 'Silences', and 'Distances', poetry has ceased to be an exercise in learned and esoteric snobbery or privacy; it is henceforth a means of simply describing popular feelings and aspirations in the idiom of the people.[1]

This chapter enters the long-running debate about Okigbo's published oeuvre and the place of 'Path of Thunder' in the compilation called *Labyrinths*. The chapter does not set out to directly prove or disprove that Okigbo saw them as separate works: it is more concerned with the evaluation of arguments regarding the compatibility and incompatibility of his earlier and later work, and to suggest another pathway by which it is possible to read the later collection 'Path of Thunder'. The chapter uses Ruth Finnegan's insights about the freelance poet as a template for the assessment of Okigbo's 'performance' as a poet. Beginning with her insights the discussion proceeds to a close reading of selected poems, examining their employment of traditional African tools, motifs, and strategies. The chapter contends that Okigbo is a much more dynamic poet than is generally believed: much time is spent examining some of the strategies at work in his later poetry. Overall the chapter seeks to broaden the debate so that less attention or blame is laid at Okigbo's feet and more emphasis is placed on such questions as artistic freedom, motivation, audience, and mask-wearing. The

1 Sunday Anozie, *Christopher Okigbo; Creative Rhetoric* (London: Evans Brothers Limited, 1972) 178.

previous chapter's discussion of Brathwaite's *X/Self* experiment revealed the challenges it posed to the poet, the reader, and the collection that housed it: this chapter in many respects conducts a similar investigation. In both instances it is apparent that these poets were responding to the current social and political climate: it is also apparent that they wrestled with their own souls as they produced their most ambitious and challenging work. Despite their many similarities, Okigbo and Brathwaite are evidently different, as has been revealed many times throughout this work. Although Brathwaite imaged the horrors of past and present terror, death, and genocide in his *X/Self,* he was not faced directly with the same dreadful dilemma that haunted Okigbo. Many of the atrocities that *X/Self* represents are set on a grand scale. Okigbo's apocalypse engulfs a wide community as well, but its greater immediate threat makes it much more unnerving than Brathwaite's treatment. Okigbo uses the past and present continuous tenses to potent effect in his 'Path of Thunder', and this and other literary and rhetorical devices serve to situate the reader in the heat and heart of the engulfing turmoil that would eventually end in death.

1. 'Path of Thunder': the Crisis of Inclusion/Exclusion Critical Approaches

The elements which were so ever-present at the beginning of Okigbo's initiation are even more potent in the concluding section 'Path of Thunder'. One might compare the 'rays, violet and short' and the storm imagery of 'Heavensgate' with the pending apocalypse that haunts 'Path of Thunder', and consider them as comprising Okigbo's total testament. The foreboding atmosphere that gave birth to the initiate's awareness of his soul's delinquency in 'Heavensgate' ('the stars have departed') threatens with equal portent in the poem 'Thunder Can Break'. The voices of wisdom and prophecy which informed the listener in earlier segments such as Upandru's with its sage instructions, or that in ('Limits' VIII) which speaks the language of war and confrontation, are still heard in 'Path of Thunder', and now conjointly as well: 'But already the hunters are talking about / pumpkins: If they share the meat let them / remember thunder.'[2]

The symbols of the 'drum', the 'labyrinth', of ominous 'birds' and other supernatural forces maintain their significance and achieve an even greater symbolic scope within the structure of the final book 'Path of Thunder'. The reader is quite sure that the character who presages an imminent death throughout the sequence of elegies in 'Path of Thunder' is the same person as the one whom the initiate represents within the earlier parts of *Labyrinths*. The musical motifs also persist; they are given added ranges of interpretation, and in turn sound new dimensions to the earlier strains. The 'lament' in 'Silences' becomes the 'Elegy' in 'Path of Thunder', and the message of the 'slit-drum' with its 'condolences' reinforces the symbolic potency of the 'long-drum' in 'Silences'. The level of sustained social commitment that inspires 'Distances' (but which hitherto had not been noticed in the religious sequences 'Heavensgate' and 'Limits') is continued right into 'Path of Thunder', hardly relenting or allowing for a moment of respite, as the division within 'Silences' had.

Ime Ikiddeh also sees similar associations between 'Path of Thunder' and the other poems:

> 'Path of Thunder' is the great triumph of Okigbo's poetry in that it marks ... the prodigal's ultimate homecoming, and it is a homecoming where

2 Christopher Okigbo, *Labyrinths* (London: Heinemann Educational Books, 1971) 67.

> the protagonist is no longer 'the sole witness' because of his felt for and now found audience.[3]

For Udoeyop 'Path of Thunder' represents another personal testimony to a current public situation[4] like those he sees in 'Limits' and 'Silences'. In addition, most of the criticisms which have offered the view that 'Path of Thunder' is related to the other sections often turn to 'Silences' for their key instances, due to that section's wealth of associative references and features. The presentation of the Franciscan nuns of 'Silences' as symbols of a society at the brink of political and social inundation is not that far removed from the turmoil being adumbrated in 'Path of Thunder'. The structural incorporation of 'crier' and 'chorus' into 'Silences' can be seen to prepare the audiences for the type of interactive performance which 'Path of Thunder' invites; and the allusion in ('Silences' II) to the death of Zaire's first president Patrice Lumumba is (as Nwoga reminds us) a prelude to the growing concern with politics and public matters which becomes predominant in 'Path of Thunder'.

Within the poet's supplication to the Earth Mother in 'Elegy for Alto' Ikiddeh sees Okigbo's 'Last Testament' in the 'Earth unbind me' prayer, suggesting that 'in the pathos of the cry we see the protagonist who in the first poem of "Heavensgate" had stood before Mother Idoto a penitent prodigal seeking guidance and protection now opting to be a prodigal again'.[5] Although one might not totally agree with the final conclusion offered, this quotation is quite significant since it is representative of the type of holistic-cum-comparative ad-hominem-tinged criticism which abounds and which tends to portray a radical embracing and abandonment of positions by the poet. This impression of

3 Ime Ikiddeh, 'Iron, Thunder and Elephants: A Study of Okigbo's "Path of Thunder"', *Critical Perspectives on Christopher Okigbo*, ed. Donatus Nwoga (Washington: Three Continents Press, 1984) 191.

4 N. J. Udoeyop, 'Okigbo: A Branch of Giant Fennel', *Critical Perspectives* 168.

5 Ikiddeh, 'Iron, Thunder and Elephants' 191.

the poet is also conveyed in sections of Chinweizu's criticism of Okigbo, whom he is at great pains to categorise as 'the early Okigbo' and 'the later Okigbo'. For Chinweizu, the early Okigbo is seen within 'the first floundering steps of "Heavensgate"', the later Okigbo is marked by his transformation in the final section 'Path of Thunder': Oyeniyi Okunoye seems to agree with this categorization.[6]

When Anozie argues against the inclusion of the 'Path of Thunder' sequence in the Heinemann collection *Labyrinths*, he is representing yet another critical approach to Okigbo – one which is segmental in outlook. His is an argument, as he says, 'from a purely literary standpoint', and this approach to Okigbo's work is also shared by Okunoye. Anozie goes on to argue:

> I don't think that *Labyrinths* and 'Path of Thunder' hang together thematically: in fact, the latter begins a new sequence altogether which Chris had probably hoped to complete in '67 or '68 and also publish in a separate volume. To publish them now together looks like it'll distort the original thematic perspective in *Labyrinths* described by Chris himself as 'a fable of man's perennial quest for fulfillment', (ii) Chris has offered us in the *Labyrinths* Ms a carefully annotated selection of his own poetry and this I think is ideal for your present purpose; in other words, conscious of this more formal public debut, he has chosen and dressed himself in his best clothes and certainly would not like anything else to be tagged on to him at this stage.[7]

Anozie uses the 'No in thunder' motif of 'Silences' to conclude that Okigbo had not fully within himself resolved the question of whether art and politics should or should not be separated.

6 Chinweizu et al., *Towards the Decolonization of African Literature* (Washington: Howard University Press, 1983) 196. Also see Oyeniyi Okunoye's essay 'Captives of Empire: Early Ibadan Poets and Poetry'. *African Study Monograph*, 19. 3 (November, 1998): 161–170.

7 Anozie, *Creative Rhetoric* 173. Okunoye's essay 'Captives of Empire: Early Ibadan Poets and Poetry' expresses a similar opinion, especially on pages 167–170.

2. (Finnegan and) Reading Okigbo as a Freelance Poet

There is indeed good literary reason for Anozie's mistrust. However, one must employ with caution those approaches that become excessively obsessed with the dictates of textual form and thematic propinquity. Suffice it to say that 'Path of Thunder' reveals a dynamic poetic attitude: it manifests a radical sequence (in the political sense) much more forthright than the obscurantist verse in 'Heavensgate', 'Limits', and 'Distances'. Certainly its reliance on folk forms and its being targeted at the folk consciousness are examples of the dynamic quality of the poet and his works: such an appraisal deliberately eschews many of the preconceived notions about the need for and pre-eminence of thematic and stylistic unity, notions which often define the thrust of formal criticism. Such an approach can overlook the question of artistic freedom and fulfilment, and can also disregard the deeper significance of the African/Igbo artistic background and context to the poetry.

I would contend that other considerations can help us to understand the poetry and the poet himself. The freelance poet of West African culture is described by Finnegan as someone who 'moves from place to place according to where he can find a wealthy patron or audience prepared to reward him in return for his poems'.[8] If one is prepared to begin to see the poet as a dynamic individual then perhaps one might read Okigbo and his poetry, especially 'Path of Thunder', differently. This is not an attempt to determine whether 'Path of Thunder' should or should not be issued along with the other sections; rather, I wish to offer an alternative approach: not totally new, but different from that of the established critical voices mentioned above. To see Okigbo as the freelance poet (as described by

8 Ruth Finnegan, *Oral Literature in Africa* (Nairobi: Oxford University Press, 1970) 92.

Finnegan)[9] is to undermine the pre-eminence assigned to textual wholeness and order which has oriented many criticisms, and to begin to foreground the poet's dynamic range of performance as an equally pertinent consideration.

To see Okigbo as a freelance poet is to accord him a much more fluid disposition. He cannot be simply labelled within a binary categorization of 'the early Okigbo' and/vs 'the later Okigbo'; there is much more intricacy in his work and personality. Closer examination of his poetry reveals the extent of its fluidity, development, and complexity.

In his interviews Okigbo was quite clear about what he wanted most from his writings up to 'Distances'. His greatest 'reward' was to be read and understood by an audience somewhere which would share his emotions.[10] Without the benefit of an interview or direct statement about 'Path of Thunder' due to the tragedy of Nigeria in 1966, one can only speculate about the 'reward' which the poet sought when he wrote this, his final sequence. He could very well have imagined his audience as comprising fellow Nigerians, Igbos. He would have them fight next to him. His fellow Nigerians were perceived as having the most to offer, hence his adoption of the indigenous voice. His employment of African and Western references in 'Heavensgate', 'Limits', and so on similarly appealed to all those who struggled internally with a divided consciousness. Given the deeply contemplative and psychological nature of this complex, his poetry in the earlier sections reflected the tortured, contorted form of his repressed anxiety. This quality remained in his poetry throughout and into 'Path of Thunder'; in the same way it can be argued that the apocalyptic atmosphere of 'Path of Thunder' reaches back to the earlier sections of 'Heavensgate'.

9 Finnegan, *Oral Literature* 92.

10 Christopher Okigbo, Interview with Louis Nkosi in *Critical Perspectives*, ed. Nwoga, 239.

As in all social and human systems, conditions and situations change over time. When later events of the Biafran war impacted his nation, he was likewise affected. For the freelance artist the practice of mask-wearing has less to do with total abandonment of an old self for a new self and more to do with adapting one's craft in response to perceived demands. His people needed him. Had he lived longer, and were he to feel again that his audience had changed, then Christopher Okigbo would have assumed another mask; and there would be no incongruity in this act, for such is the norm for the freelance poet.

3. Reading 'Path of Thunder'

'Path of Thunder' represents Okigbo's response to the series of events in Nigeria from late 1965 until about the middle of 1966. With the exception of 'Elegy of the Wind' each of the poems in the six-poem sequence can be dated: 'Come Thunder', written one month before the military coup; 'Hurrah for Thunder' written a day after it; and 'Thunder Can Break', 'Elegy for Slit-Drum', and 'Elegy for Alto' (all written some five months after the coup). In these one can trace the development of events and the poet's personal and artistic responses to these developments.

In 'Path of Thunder' Christopher Okigbo is no more committed to his craft than in any of the other sections from 'Heavensgate' to 'Distances'. What has changed here, rather, is his perception of and response to a new audience. The court poet of the earlier segments gives way to 'the people's poet' in 'Path of Thunder', and Okigbo signals this movement at the conclusion of 'Hurrah for Thunder':

If I don't learn to shut my mouth I'll soon go to hell,
I, Okigbo, town-crier, together with my iron bell.[11]

At the outset of the above poem an 'elephant' lies stricken; in a sense the poet is attempting to maintain some degree of mystery and indirectness – features that were associated with his earlier myth-tinged verse. But as well, and more importantly, he is employing an indigenous symbol (the elephant), a part of the traditional hunter's list of prized game, as part of his poetry. 'Hurrah for Thunder' is Okigbo's 'Hunting Song'. Such songs were often sung to celebrate the capturing of game considered to be particularly awesome and potent. Okigbo saw the appropriateness of employing the metaphor of hunting in reference to military activity because of his understanding of the relatedness between hunting poetry and military poetry: both are associated (as Finnegan notes) 'with the ideas of danger, pride and glory'.[12] These are sung usually in anticipation of confrontation; but they are also sung vociferously on completion of a successful mission. In 'Hurrah for Thunder' Christopher Okigbo mirrors the practice where 'a hunter is expected to climb on to the body of an elephant and burst into song':[13]

Hurrah for thunder ...
Hurrah for thunder ...[14]

Okigbo's chorus (of voices) becomes like the heroic hunter's song of north-east Africa:

1st chorus: He has slain / he has destroyed him.

2nd chorus: Whither went he when he slew him?

1st chorus: As he went hence did I see him at all?

11 Okigbo, *Labyrinths* 67.
12 Finnegan, *Oral Literature* 221.
13 Finnegan, *Oral Literature* 222.
14 Okigbo, *Labyrinths* 67.

All: Perhaps on the bank of the river he has stricken him down. Destroyer and slayer art thou called, Hurray, Hurrah, doubly a slayer.[15]

Okigbo has also added the most essential component of the hunting song; that is, an impressive description of the prey. Babalola's list of actual praise names given to these beasts is also echoed in Okigbo's verse. Babalola's list tells of 'Elephant praise-named: He-who-used-his-hand-as-a-trumpet, Elephant called: He-who-remains-mountainous-even-when-seated'.[16] Consider Okigbo's

The elephant, tetrach of the jungle:
With a wave of the hand
He could pull four trees to the ground;
His four mortar legs pounded the earth:
Wherever they treaded,
The grass was forbidden to be there.[17]

This serves to re-emphasize the prowess of the hunter, as Finnegan notes;[18] but for Okigbo it is principally a useful metaphor for describing the ominous threat to a society's rights. The beast's threat to 'the ground', 'the earth', and 'the grass' (all sacred, and symbols of life and growth) effectively conveys this reality. Okigbo is now less concerned with the myth than he is with the metaphor; and the means for interpreting and going beyond its surface level rely on an awareness of the distinctly indigenous African input which is that submerged half (and yet everything). The elephant here is Sir Abubakar Tafawa Balewa, the Federal Prime Minister who was killed on the night of 15 January 1966 by a group of young officers in response to what

15 H. M. Chadwick, *The Growth of Literature*, 3 vols. (London: Cambridge, 1932–40) Vol. 3: 514.
16 S. A Babalola, 'The Characteristic Features of Outer Form of Yoruba Ijala Chants', *Odu* 1.1–2 (1964–65): 51.
17 Okigbo, *Labyrinths* 67.
18 Finnegan, *Oral Literature* 223.

they interpreted as his repressive rule. Okigbo has also alluded to other political and social figures and their function through related devices. In 'Elegy for Slit-Drum' the 'General' is General Aguiyi-Ironsi, who unceremoniously unseats the young officers of the 15 January coup. Symbolically, 'an iron mask covers his face'[19] indicating his pernicious disposition, evil intent, and perhaps also, as Fraser intimates, a premonition that 'the cruel face of human history' promises 'retribution and mutual destruction'.[20] He is eventually disposed of as well.

A similar prophetic caution haunts much of Okigbo's so-called celebratory/militant verse in 'Path of Thunder'. In 'Hurrah for Thunder' Okigbo cautions the masses:

> But already the hunters are talking about pumpkins:
> If they share the meat let them remember thunder.[21]

This air of uncertainty and pending doom lurks within every path: it informs the poet's delivery and re-emphasizes the poem's sense of timelessness and its cyclical portrayal of tragedy, partial respite, and eternal tension. All this gives resonance to the universal statement that the town crier can be seen to make in 'Path of Thunder'. His becomes a warning to all mankind about the potential for evil within all human transactions, whether they be political or spiritual. It offers little comfort, but provides much wisdom in the revelation that:

> AN OLD STAR departs, leaves us here on the shore
> Gazing heavenward for a new star approaching;
> The new star appears, foreshadows its going
> Before a going and coming that goes on forever ...[22]

19 Okigbo, *Labyrinths* 69.

20 Robert Fraser, *West African Poetry* (Cambridge: Cambridge University Press, 1986) 135.

21 Okigbo, *Labyrinths* 67.

22 Okigbo, *Labyrinths* 72.

Okigbo's supplanting the myth with the metaphor is not so much a conscious attempt at stylistic transformation; rather, this transformation is an accompanying feature of Okigbo's most recent poetic stance. The need to reach and communicate primarily with a home audience has given birth to a mode of expression which derives much influence from the form, structure, content, and effect of the proverb and its associated verbal forms. 'Hurrah for Thunder' presents the most direct employment of the proverb in all of 'Path of Thunder':

> The eye that looks down will surely see the nose;
> The finger that fits should be used to pick the nose.[23]

But this direct borrowing is only a sample of the weight that the proverb carries within 'Path of Thunder'. Proverbs are capable of many functions, and are equally diverse in terms of the form which they might take; but in the final analysis they represent 'the soul of a people'. The folk-infused tone which Okigbo's 'Path of Thunder' achieves, that quality which perhaps is more often alluded to in criticism than concretely identified, owes much to the stylistics associated with proverbs within West African society: contrast, the hyperbole, and equivocation are three of these features which become significant to our analysis here. But in addition, other more subtle attributes of the proverb will be seen to be employed by the town crier for this, his most recent assignment.

The poem's warning about retributionand time's cyclical nature and its recommendation of cautious rejoicing are aptly conveyed in the work's most obvious proverb (quoted above). It is aptly placed as a reminder after the description of the euphoric jubilation ('Hurrah ...') that is about to inundate a nation just one day after a popular coup. Such a caution had already been lodged in the lines of the same poem:

23 Okigbo, *Labyrinths* 67.

> But already the hunters are talking about pumpkins:
> If they share the meat let them remember thunder.[24]

The message is the same in both cases; but what we have here is a rare occasion where Okigbo reinforces his message to the public, firstly through the medium of the allegory, then by use of the proverb. This device has the dual effect of giving a clue to the interpretation of Okigbo's allegory, as well as relaying its message to a particular audience, those for whom the proverb is an esoteric means of communication.

Okigbo's engagement with proverbs did not begin with 'Path of Thunder'. As I have intimated before, he is a much more dynamic poet than he is sometimes credited with being. The proverb first gains employment in 'Initiations' ('Heavensgate'), in the word of the half-demented minstrel Jadum. His proverbs seemed less instruction or wisdom than the irrational utterances of a nocturnal screamer. They were re-presented primarily (one feels) to give substance to a character whom the poet knew as a boy rather than for any cathartic purposes. It is with Upandru that the proverb began to achieve the importance and relevance that it would later take on in 'Path of Thunder'. The proverbial sayings of ('Limits' VI) are foremost a biblical echo which further complicates, as opposed to explaining, the mysteries of the ministrant's relationship both to art and to his society. Upandru's catechism with its induced answers foreshadows the type of response that the poet wishes to achieve from the reader. Where Upandru's playful indulgence had led to the central clue for decoding the labyrinth ('except by rooting') the poet now seeks to achieve a similar rapport between himself and his audience, whom he hopes will pass his message on.

What is most interesting, however, are the similarities in form shared by the proverbs and Okigbo's style as he attempts to take his message to the masses. In 'Come Thunder' 'Remember ... Remember' appears as a warning, a caution unto

24 Okigbo, *Labyrinths* 67.

wisdom – which is what a proverb is all about. While a proverb is often succinct and lucid through some logical association or dissociation, Okigbo uses contrast to create a similar sobering effect within his verse. The jubilant 'dancers' are contrasted with 'the thunder among the clouds', and later they appear counterpositioned against 'the lightning beyond the earth'. Although written one month before the coup, this poem is like 'Hurrah for Thunder' (a post-coup piece) in terms of its ambivalence towards the goings-on within society.

The copious reference to animals within this section of the poetry also enhances its make-up of traditional elements. The assumption being made here, of course, is that within traditional society there is a closer association between the person and his/her natural world, which is not that far removed from their habitat. This phenomenon has shaped the Igbo view about nature, the animals, and the relationship which man shares with them in a cosmos whose equilibrium relies on their mutual coexistence. Finnegan buttresses this perception through an explanation of how animals can be used within proverbs to expound/reveal some truth or matter to humankind, she suggests that 'proverbs about animals are very common indeed ... as in the tales about animals and in certain praise names, a comment is often being made about human life and action through references to non-human activity.[25] In 'Elegy for Slit-Drum' one observes:

> the elephant ravages the jungle
> the jungle is peopled with snakes
> the snake says to the squirrel
> I will swallow you
> the mongoose says to the snake

25 Finnegan, *Oral Literature* 396.

I will mangle you
the elephant says to the mongoose
I will strangle you ...[26]

This could be taken directly from the pages of a tale about animals or from an associated folk-tale source. Here is an example of the close relationship that Okigbo's verse can have with his own indigenous tradition. The idea being communicated here is one of a 'cut-throat' social order. The predominant image is one of perpetual and perennial confrontation, which is conveyed by the systematic process of engulfing and being engulfed: 'the squirrel', then 'the snake', then 'the mongoose', and 'the elephant'. This shows a sound knowledge of the animal world, and espouses the philosophy of survival of the fittest. In a deeper sense this is a representation of Okigbo's society in crisis as he saw it on that bleak afternoon in May 1966, some five months after the coup and General Ironsi's usurpation of power from the young officers. Okigbo has reproduced to the Igbo masses a portrait of their 'dog-eat-dog' world. Finally, a tinge of humour is attempted, as is characteristic of any good storyteller whose final line can be as humourous as it is ironic – and poignant. After the portrayal of ongoing power struggles:

thunder fells the trees cut a path
thunder smashes them all – condolences ...[27]

The poet's employment of the allegorical mode partly explains his adoption of what Finnegan terms 'a specialized and extreme form' of expression, where 'the speaker wishes to convey something, but in such a way that later on he can deny that he actually stated what was implied.'[28] In 'Path of Thunder' the allegory and metaphor have the effect of creating wider im-

26 Okigbo, *Labyrinths* 70.
27 Okigbo, *Labyrinths 70.*
28 Finnegan, *Oral Literature* 411.

plications of meaning. In 'Elegy for Alto' the actors are, plainly, 'the robbers', 'the Eagles', and the political figures appear without even the distinction of a definite article: they are, obscurely, 'politicians'. No one (no regime) can say that Christopher Okigbo has pointed his finger at them. This is more a part of Okigbo's attempt, one thinks, at self-preservation and an indication of his shrewd artistry, than it is a signal of his uncertainty about his commitment and about how far the artist should go without abandoning his personal voice in favour of politics and polemics. 'Path of Thunder' can ultimately take on local and universal significance. Yes, it is about the specific events in Nigeria; but it is also about the condition of the world.

What is also noteworthy about Okigbo's method in 'Path of Thunder' is his conscious use of repetition and versal parallelism (where an entire line or a significant part thereof is repeated or counterbalanced): both of these features are acknowledged to be distinguishing traits within traditional West African oratory and versification. The following translation of an original Igbo prayer to a dead father provides an opportunity for critical comparison with a segment of Okigbo's work in 'Path of Thunder':

> My Father
> I have brought this dog to you
> When you are reborn
> Slay not your children
> And may they not slay you.
> May you kill none by accident
> But may you kill your enemies with intent.
> My Father
> I am sacrificing this cock to you
> When you are reborn
> may your ikenga stand straight.[29]

Prior to the conclusion of 'Elegy for Slit-Drum' we read:

29 Ulli Beier, *Python; Ibo Poetry* (Port Moresby: Papua Pocket Poets, 1967) 17.

THUNDER that has struck the elephant
the same thunder should wear a plume – condolences

a roadmaker makes a road
the road becomes a throne
can we cane him for felling a tree – condolences

THUNDER that has struck the elephant
the same thunder can make a bruise – condolences.[30]

Although the latter poem is in no way a prayer – and is thematically distinct – it is associated with the former in that both are recited on the occasion of death. Whereas the former strikes a chord of reverence, the latter is heavy with both caution and irony. But they are more alike at the level of rendering, and more specifically in terms of structural form. 'My Father' is the dominant motif in the Igbo prayer, not solely because it is to him that the prayer is being addressed, but because of the father's elevated status which is reasserted through the constant repetition of his title. 'Thunder' also achieves this central focus on account of its repetition in 'Elegy for Slit-Drum'. It is therefore established as that thing to be considered most; hence its potency can never be overlooked, a potency which is reinforced by the paying and repaying of condolences to its victims. Repetition also takes on the form of versal repetition: in the Igbo prayer above the line 'when you are reborn' is repeated in its entirety, and the clause 'I have brought this dog to you' is echoed seven lines later in 'I am sacrificing this cock to you'. In Okigbo's 'Elegy for Slit-Drum' similar stylistic features appear. Direct repetition is given to 'thunder that has struck the elephant', whereas its supporting clauses on each occasion are rendered with slight adjustments:

Thunder that has struck the elephant
the same thunder should wear a plume – condolences…

30 Okigbo, *Labyrinths* 70.

Thunder that has struck the elephant
the same thunder can make a bruise – condolences[31]

In addition to maintaining a stanzaic balance these devices have the distinctive effect of creating the tone and cadence of rhetorical verse, a form that according to Finnegan is often held to be a salient feature of traditional West African versification.

The associated stylistic feature of parallelism pervades the poem, where it has the effect of conveying the intensity of the tongue/message/speech of the slit-drum:

condolences from our split-tongue of the slit drum condolences

one tongue full of fire
one tongue full of stone … [32]

A measure of tension is communicated firstly through the lyrics of the verse. One tongue of the slit-drum is 'full of fire' while the other is 'full of stone', suggesting both ardent outcry/protest and hard/harsh censorship. Its parallel structure helps to emphasize the close relationship between the tongues:

one tongue ...

one tongue ...

They are one in purpose and voice, the one depending on the other, the one supporting the other: but the juxtaposing of what must be their conflicting message is particularly bothering,[33] and tellingly symbolic of the competing and often conflicting demands of society (public concerns) and artistry (private concerns) upon the poet.

Judging from the absence of criticism on the nature and function of rhythm in 'Path of Thunder' it would seem that

31 Okigbo, *Labyrinths* 70.
32 Okigbo, *Labyrinths* 68.
33 As F. Bebey says, 'the [slit] drum which announces happy events is not used to spread news of deaths', see Bebey, *African Music* 96.

rhythm is more overtly sounded and suggested within the titles of the poems ('Elegy for Slit-Drum'; 'Elegy for Alto') than within the actual verse. But careful scrutiny reveals otherwise, for Okigbo is as committed to experimenting with the poetic tool of rhythm as are some exponents within the oral tradition. The rhythm that permeates 'Path of Thunder' has very much to do with some of the features explored earlier, such as repetition; but in addition it has to do with the poem's structure on the page and the associations (with music and rhythm) that the poet implies within the titles of his poems.

The rhythmic variations within 'Path of Thunder' are influential determinants of the moods that interplay within this section. Like some traditional exponents who could sway the emotions of their audience through tampering with rhythm, the modern town crier of 'Path of Thunder' has produced verse that can be described as incantatory, intense, meditative, choral, monophonic, and polyphonic.

The incantatory quality of 'Come Thunder' derives partly from its repetition of identical phrases. These phrases are enhanced by a versal arrangement that allows for the poem's performance by two or more voices. Within the first five lines there is an alternating rhythm which is intimated simply by the structured layout of lines on the page: the longer line is followed by a shorter one. A more technical analysis reveals one heavily pulsed line giving way to a less heavily pulsed one. The sense of rhythm in 'Hurrah for Thunder' is dictated by simple punctuation. The rhythmic pattern of the final eight lines (for example) is suggested by the use of the colon, semicolon, comma, and full stop, which represent different lengths of pause:

> But already the hunters are talking about pumpkins:
> If they share the meat let them remember thunder–
>
> The eye that looks down will surely see the nose;
> The finger that fits should be used to pick the nose.

Today-for tomorrow, today becomes yesterday:
How many million promises can ever fill a basket.

If I don't learn to shut my mouth I'll soon go to hell,
I, Okigbo, town-crier/ together with my iron bell.[34]

The first line of each two-line stanza offers a break in rhythm: only the duration of a colon, semi-colon, or comma, but (for the most part) it is not until the end of each stanza that the rhythm is actually seen to stop. The corresponding lines of each stanza are basically of identical length, metre, and rhythm, except for the rhythmic variations within lines 5 and 8 when the comma intervenes. Performance notation is therefore written into the page. Each line within the two-line stanza depends on the other for full meaning, and for resolution. Significantly also, any one of these verses can exist without the other.

'Elegy for Alto' and 'Elegy for Slit-Drum' re-emphasize the oral qualities within 'Path of Thunder'. 'Elegy for Slit-Drum' is perhaps the most rhythmically dynamic of all the poems in 'Path of Thunder'. When Nketia makes the point that in Africa the music of a two- or three-tone instrument (like the slit-drum) may be effective 'if it has a strong rhythmic influence',[35] some conscious understanding of that phenomenon on Okigbo's part becomes evident from a reading of 'Elegy for Slit-Drum'. Its haunting repetitive lines of 'condolences' are given the notation of 'diminuendo' by the centre of the poem where they fade, only to return with greater intensity and heavier accent, reaching a crescendo by the final two lines:

trunk of the iron tree we cry *condolences* when we break,
shells of the open sea we cry *condolences* when we shake ...[36]

34 Okigbo, *Labyrinths* 67.
35 J. H. Nketia, *The Music of Africa* (London: Gallancz, 1975) 125.
36 Okigbo, *Labyrinths* 70.

That polyrhythmic texture, which Chernoff[37] highlights as a characteristic of all African vocal compositions that make use of alternating voices of chorus and soloist, is evident within 'Elegy for Slit-Drum'. The chorus's voices can be made to intone all those lines that offer 'condolences', whereas the soloist recites all the others. This can have the effect of creating a counter-movement of tone and rhythm, when after the chorus's single line

> Condolences ... from our swollen lips laden with condolences

there comes the soloist's double

> The mythmaker accompanies us
> The rattles are here with us ...[38]

But whereas the chorus's line maintains its basic format and structure, the soloist engages in a series of improvisations: shifting to four-line phrases, then to two lines again, to six and to eight, then back to two again: and always his rhythm is contrasted against, counterpointed by, the more rhythmically and metrically regimented cadence of each chorus:

> (Crier) The General is up... the General is up... commandments...
> the General is up the General is up the General is up –
>
> (Chorus) condolences from our twin-beaks and feathers condolences:
>
> (Crier) the General is near the throne
> an iron mask covers his face
> the General has carried the day
> the mortars are far away –

37 John Chernoff, *African Rhythm and African Sensibility* (Chicago: University of Chicago Press, 1979) 91–151.

38 Okigbo, *Labyrinths* 68.

(Chorus) condolences to appease the fever of a wake among tumbled tombs

(Crier) the elephant has fallen
the mortars have won the day
the elephant has fallen
does he deserve his fate
the elephant has fallen
can we remember the date –[39]

Primarily 'Path of Thunder' has revealed Christopher Okigbo's dynamic quality and his ability to manipulate his craft, in this case to suit the principal demands of addressing an indigenous audience. He has shown a keen perception of the workings of folk life and of the folk mind, a knowledge which has thrown up a number of salient similarities of style between his work and that of the traditional folk poet / town crier. For Joe Ushie this is not a radical departure for poets like Okigbo, since he considers Okigbo's contemporaries to have been responding to their social and personal realities.[40] Arguably, there is no other African poet whose oeuvre has stirred such competing critiques. Maybe Alex Irvine touches the mark when, commenting on the competing contentious critical positions, he remarks that 'for one biographical critic he is a Jungian intellectual, for another a proletarian revolutionary; and on and on. This violent disagreement speaks to the importance of both Okigbo himself and the myth his death has made possible'.[41] For me the poet's death has helped to empower the mystique surrounding his

39 Okigbo, *Labyrinths* 69.

40 Joe Ushie, 'Phases in Nigerian Poetry in English'. n.d. <http://64.233.169.104/search?q=cache:wuPEHw4FYm8J: www.africaresearch.org/Papers/N05/Ush1.pdf+okigbo+path+of+thunder+and+earlier+poetry&hl=en&ct=clnk&cd=18>. Accessed July 21, 2007.

41 Alex Irvine, 'Postcolonial Generations: Yeats and Okigbo'. n.d. <http://64.233.169.104/search?q=cache:VZeOUjxqL0J:www.alexirvine.net/okigbo.pdf+okigbo+path+of+thunder+and+earlier+poetry&hl=en&ct=clnk&cd=13>. Accessed July 21, 2007.

work. But even more so it is his poetry that has provoked such debate. It is its dynamic quality that intrigues some and repulses others – readers and critics alike. It is the resolute craftsman, the freelance spirit, who fashions this poetry, making it hard to finally pin down and label. In 'Path of Thunder' and *X/Self* the poets stand at the threshold. They look backwards on to a past of personal and collective crisis, and they peer tentatively into the future: it is hardly any different. As the two collections come to an end, darkness is coming in.

POSTLUDE

Okigbo and Brathwaite in Cyberspace: Technology: Literature: Being Digital

This book has examined the creative work of a specific period: it has considered contemporary commentary on that work, but the focus has always returned to older seminal critical statements to help ground the discourse. This final chapter is different in many ways. It belongs to the rest of the study, but it also looks ahead to other kinds of discourses that are possible in evaluating artists of the predigital era. This chapter is partly motivated by my own interest in cyberculture studies, but its more significant impetus derives from the need to expand literary criticism in this area, which is still too often tied to conventional approaches and media (especially in the Caribbean and African academies). I hope that my work can offer new perspectives and findings, but can also reveal the limitations and challenges of so-called 'new' approaches/readings. Whatever the outcome, it must be acknowledged that the process offers its own rewards.

The expansion of debate to include new and emerging media does not signify a sacrilegious desecration of literary studies, rather it acknowledges that there are new literacies, that the Internet is pivotally placed, and that new media are destined to interact more and more with traditional ones. This final chapter therefore opens up the debate and raises questions some of which it does not or cannot definitively answer. In as much as Okigbo and Brathwaite are regarded as experimental and frontier artists in their own right, it is intriguing to consider how their work and their iconography are played out in certain sectors of cyberspace, which after all represents the cusp of our experiential reality.

Most of this book has engaged with work produced in the 1960s, some forty years ago. What has become obvious, however, is that in spite of this fact the issues and concerns raised by these artists are very current today. A critical analysis of that work from our contemporary vantage point has certainly served to recast the work, as though it were being rewritten for our time. The filter or perspective or medium that one uses for assessing cultural material very often has the potential to rejuvenate even re-originate that work. For instance, Brathwaite's reissuing of the *The Arrivants* as a digital audio text has given that a sort of separate existence: even the 1960s Decca/Argo analogue production is not the same as the post-2000 digitally remastered product. Hardcore literary buffs will say that the text of the two versions is no different, and all that has taken place is a process of transferral from one medium/format to another, from vinyl to compact disc. But a clearer grasp of concepts like mastering and remastering sheds greater light on this subject and provides keener insight into my way of coming to culture and cultural recordings.

The notion of an original master document or recording serves as a point of reference for understanding what a remaster is. The master recording is usually the definitive finished copy of a work, from which copies are often made. In theory this is how the process is supposed to work, but in practice it does not always flow in this way. While 'digital remastering' became a buzzword in the late 1980s and the 1990s, there were in fact several processes that defined how remastered copies related to the master. In some instances duplication was done off of an edited (cleaned up) version of the original master copy: very often remastering involved the use of several editing tools that encode equalization, compression, and maximization into the original master copy. As a result, you can never be really sure how versions and their masters relate to each other.

Given the intervention of technology within the process of copying and proliferation, I am inclined to suggest that versions like Brathwaite's post-2000 *The Arrivants* (compact disc) have been encoded with several layers of technology. It is these technical layers rather than any overt tampering that makes the work a potentially different kind of text.

I have for some time suggested that technology's imprint on culture and cultural data is more significant than we tend to believe. By this I mean that we often take technology's doings for granted. We have become so used to its presence in our daily lives that we often overlook or underestimate its influence. In this book I have therefore taken some care in indicating whether my analysis of the poets' work was based on the traditional printed text or some other version. While I did not concern myself excessively with the question of the various versions produced by the poets, there is, of course, sufficient material to allow for a protracted debate at some other time, or in another forum. As has been indicated within previous chapters, critics of the work of the two poets have over time discussed the issue of versions, unity and disunity of the text, and the extent to which the authors and their publishers seemed comfortable with their work: we may say that there is already substantial discussion about that issue.

Partly for that reason I do not want to enter the debate at that level. I would rather point to the fact that both Okigbo and Brathwaite are like the tracks of data that define their work. They are as potentially diverse. This is an easy point to grasp if you consider the fact that critics have for some time spoken of two Okigbos – the sophisticated artist, and the town crier of the later period. My approach, however, wants to take this type of analysis a little further. I want to suggest that Okigbo and Brathwaite (and by extension their work) can be considered as having yet another set of dimensions/realities because they are – in this era – digital beings. They could not exist digitally until the age of digital reality was ushered in, but the rapid changes in technology that affected all spheres of human life during the last two decades of the twentieth century have also affected the beings we are. The post-twentieth-century virtual culture matrix also breathed new identities and ideas into our consciousness, creating and recreating several versions of our selves. Poets like Okigbo and Brathwaite were reborn in new ways when the Internet emerged, proliferated, and took over the role of defining who we are. Virtual media did not just offer another version of the original, it presented numerous copies. Prior to virtual technologies like the Internet, it was not possible to locate so many simulations of an artist in a specified space. Okigbo and Brathwaite therefore exist within the machine (technology) in several versions. Since innumerable representation is possible in cyberspace, one can get a grip on this situation by considering some of the various kinds of cyber locations and sites that have gone about the process of projecting versions of the poets. This can allow one to imagine how the numerous simulations are constituted; and it also shows up the imperfections and inadequacies of reaching for identity compression (consolidation) in digital space.

There is significant data to be gained from an exploratory analysis of how these two poets and their lives and work have become re-energized/recast as a result of being beamed up at several locations within the virtual-culture matrix. This analysis wants to point the way towards other kinds of similar approaches, taking into account the intersection between culture and technology.

1. Okigbo – Energize!

Whereas Okigbo died in the real world in 1967, he enjoyed a new life during the digital age. If the analogue age came to an end some time around 1990, the digital culture era went into full bloom during the 1990s. The digital era can be equated with the development and popularization of the computer and related slick-functioning machines: for some people, the computer and Internet are the defining instruments/phenomena of the digital age.

With the advent and expansion of the Internet it was possible to circumvent more traditional, cumbersome, and static ways of performing tasks. The Internet was created initially as a network to maintain communication and a way of life in the event that a nuclear war destroyed more traditional means of communication. It was associated firstly with the USA military and with a few educational institutions, but by the mid-1990s it belonged principally to commercial enterprises, groups, associations, and large financial interests and players in the Western world. In the last few years it has undergone a substantial transformation, as powerful transnational interests wrestled to retain control in the face of a growing democratization of cyberspace: it is now possible for many more people to enter the virtual domain and to conduct a range of transactions there. Because this is so, it is also more challenging to locate and conclusively define people, objects, and things in cyberspace. Poets like Okigbo are a particular challenge.

The virtual Okigbo has several locations and manifestations. Many of the websites that feature or host Okigbo or information about him belong to educational institutions, book retailers, educational publications, literary dictionaries – and some to YouTube and Weblogs. This range of locations reveals the extent to which Okigbo has evolved with time. A careful analysis of his virtual signatures reveals the extent to which he has become immortalized, given the number of sites that celebrate his heroic action to place the community's interests before his own artistic project: some conferences and fundraising activities celebrate his memory as a poet and as a patriot.

Molara Wood, a Nigerian writer and arts journalist living in London, posted on her blog around 29 April 2006 a general invitation to a fundraiser by the Christopher Okigbo Foundation.[1] No comments were posted in response to this blog announcement, but its dissemination in the blogosphere reflects the extent to which nonmainstream conduits have seized some control of information about iconic figures. Other Weblogs that feature Okigbo's work actually devote time to talking about its meaning. The GBMNews.com website is a site that has hosted information about Okigbo, including two featured articles that are highly ranked in a Google engine search for the name 'Christopher Okigbo'. This website has the subtitle 'A site for … Gay Men of colour'. The site is not fixated with Okigbo per se, rather it appears to favour giving coverage to cultural events that feature Black men. Okigbo's popularity is therefore also enhanced by such a publication, making him open to many more users, but also potentially repositioning his work and his image in cyberspace.

Many of the several video 'performances' in honour of Okigbo that appear on the Internet are hosted at YouTube, such as Achebe's address at Harvard University's Okigbo International Conference of September 2007. The YouTube phenomenon has burgeoned over the past three years. Although it plays host to a wide range of material, it is most usually categorized as appealing to young people, and is seen as one of the more visible instruments of popular culture. The finding of Okigbo there arguably places him within the arena of contemporary pop culture, signifying the extent to which Okigbo's iconography is being altered as it comes into contact with modern instruments and tools. But the discovery of Okigbo at YouTube also signifies the extent to which such pop phenomena are being infiltrated by a range of different materials and agencies:

1 Molara Wood, 'Molara Wood: The Writings of a General Wordsbody'. April 2006. <http://molarawood.blogspot.com/2006/04/mother-idoto-for-christopher-okigbo.html>. Accessed May 16, 2008.

just as being there signals the shifting of Okigbo's image, his presence also helps to alter the perception of the very medium which presents versions of his work. It should not be concluded, though, that Okigbo and his work has so infiltrated the digital culture matrix that he is now some sort of pop-culture symbol. This is not his dominant projection in cyberspace; rather, it reflects the ways in which the spaces assigned to popular youth expression are infiltrated by other kinds of activity. In a matter of years YouTube will move even closer to mainstream in terms of its users and the messages that it promotes. Private individuals and institutions are more willing today to launch a presence on YouTube than they were a few years ago. Okigbo's imprint in YouTube is more reflective of a general movement towards embracing YouTube and other kinds of popular sites, than a sign that he has become a pop symbol in the manner (say) of Bob Marley.

His daughter's website 'Christopher Okigbo Foundation' has a high search ranking <http://www.christopher-okigbo.org/>. It is an aesthetically pleasing site that presents basic information about the man, the poet, and the prophet. It is sparing in its presentation of materials. Some of the major headings for further enquiry relate to 'About Us', 'Links', 'Donations', and 'Contact Us'. The sparseness of the site is not a distraction from its visibility, as the use of earth-coloured tones supplies a texture befitting a reflective site. In spite of the fact that the foundation seeks to impel its constituents to contribute to its current needs, even that objective seems to give way to the powerful visual presence of Okigbo. This presence is taken up and beamed forward into cyberspace. On the site this presence is projected via the two photos of Okigbo, one of him lighting a pipe and the other with him peering into your eyes as you try to navigate the site. The site seems very comfortable with its project. By carefully reconstructing its imagery, foregrounding Okigbo, it seems to desire to maintain his iconic stature. And it does manage to do so. The reproduction and foregrounding of photos of Okigbo and some of his writings only recently widely published on the Internet reinforce messages concerning who he was and what he still remains. But the strategy of not giving much information, even concerning the organization at its 'About Us' link, and the replacing of that information with words from Okigbo's poetry, exposes the effort expended to keep him intact. Because it is near impossible to retain full control of one's creations and wishes in cyberspace anyway, the site turns inwards upon its own sparseness and forces the reader to go elsewhere in order to capture fuller presentations of the man and the poet.

Given the period in which he lived, it is not surprising that only a few photos of Okigbo exist. These photos have become stock signifiers of the man and the poet. If there are few images that define him, the web compensates by offering a substantial number of text-based sites. Other academics also invade the space that is Okigbo's, for instance, Ali Mazrui with his *The Trial of Christopher Okigbo*. The Web images of Okigbo are not new ones. They have appeared before on the covers of academic books and related literature, so they are known prior to their Web distribution. However, the ability that the user of the Internet has to manipulate and manage these images further reiterates the extent to which the images and who they represent can be altered, if the user of the image so desires to do, via software tools.

But one of the more exciting manifestations of Okigbo's expansive and expanding presences has to do with the publishing of works not previously in the public domain. His daughter Obiageli Okigbo kept selected rough drafts of poems written in English and Igbo, among a few other creative works. The Christopher Okigbo Foundation, which she founded in 2004, subsequently submitted these works to the UNESCO Memory of the World Register. In 2007 these rough Okigbo documents appeared at the UNESCO Memory of the World site <http://portal.unesco.org/ci/photos/showgallery.php/cat/861>.

The pieces found in the photobank there include 'Bird's Lament' and 'The Tree'. Both poems are reflective, philosophical, ceremonial, and powerful: they are not radically unlike the poems of the earlier sections of *Labyrinths*. 'The Tree' can be read as a philosophical piece. In a thought, a moment of focus upon nature, the poet provides a deeply pessimistic, if true, observation about the process of life and death. Like the tree which is born and dies at the root, so the human being is fated to return to the earth when the 'blood dries out in the vein':

> The Tree
>
> The root has struck
> A layer of rock;
>
> The sap dries out in the stem
> Upwards
>
> The blood dries out in the vein
> Like sap. (Aug 16th 1959)

These pieces do not vary the themes presented by Okigbo before. But the posting of the documents in cyberspace, as they appear at the UNESCO site, means that the pieces are in virtual position to be reread every day. The owners of these valuable documents must have wondered about how to treat them, given that Okigbo's stature has been elevated to almost mythical proportions. The decision to have them lodged with UNESCO was certainly based on the belief that its prestigious Register was a fitting place for this important African and world writer.

But there must also have been some agonizing over the techno-cultural logistics. The poems are presented as JPEG images, which means that the text of the work cannot in itself be altered, at least not easily. But the picture images can be copied from the online site by anyone who chooses to do so, hence making them the companion document for anyone who wants to lift Okigbo's hottest work into their technological possession. The Internet therefore provides wide renown for this work, but it also means that the work can be moved and virtually appropriated to other locations and contexts for fair use, but also appropriated beneath the radar of copyright. This capacity to lift, cut, and paste signals the potential for compressing Okigbo's image as a literary icon, but it also reflects digital culture's ability to decentre and diffuse by way of opening up the image to current treatments and to future (hidden) applications.

These documents are therefore leading-edge replications of the real. Because of their open display in cyberspace and the potential for wider and wider circulation, they will no doubt be asked to stand in for the originals. The storage as a JPEG picture file retains the copy as though in a picture frame. It can be looked at and read, but can't be tampered with, unless (of course) the outer frame is removed or broken. Current technology concerns itself with questions of accessing, manipulating, and owning of works. Hackers and other legitimate users of digital technology are daily engaged in various acts relating to accessing, manipulating, and gaining posession of items that they encounter in cyberspace. Formats like PDF were set up to create some measure of security for documents and to remind users that there is some distance between themselves and the particular items that they seek to make contact with in the digital matrix. Okigbo's work is destined to become even more embroiled in this kind of discursive matrix.

2. Brathwaite: YouTube: CowPasture

I have of course touched on some aspects of Kamau Bathwaite's Web presence in the book *The Politics of Caribbean Cyberculture*. I do not intend to go over that material here. I however want to consider, as I did with Okigbo, how selected copies of early

Brathwaite circulate in cyberspace, and the extent to which it might be said that the Internet spawns other versions in a way not possible before its invention.

The special claim that can be made for the Internet's unique capacity for simulation has to do with the Internet's highly complex yet flexible and dynamic make-up. Some might argue that earlier media like radio and television were also imbued with this magic, for after all television reproduced people's likenesses in a way not possible before its popularization; and there is some merit in the suggestion that the Internet is yet another invention in a succession of display media. All this is true, and in this study I have already suggested how audio versions of Brathwaite's poetry require other kinds of readings as they evoke their own responses.

The Internet's architecture, its built-in functions that allow for interactivity and communication in near real time, set it apart from other more static one-way inventions. Because any individual can enter this sphere and alter minute bits of its ever-expanding reach, this makes it an evolving entity (nearly) with a life of its own, except that it depends on individuals to contribute to its evolution. In turn, it has the capacity to project simulations of those individuals and of others, even if they are oblivious of its presence.

As with Okigbo, Brathwaite's various simulations evolve through educational sites, literary publications, commercial sales interests, and video-hosting institutions and sites. His earlier years enjoy a fair amount of attention. Sites like <www.brittanica.com> and <www.poets.org/kbrat/> recount his life and times as well as allowing their information about his upbringing and early writing years to help recast the iconic figure. As you might expect, there are more actual versions of still images of Brathwaite online than there are of Okigbo. While Okigbo has just three or four different still shots in circulation, Brathwaite's stills exceed twenty. But these are hardly really diverse images, as many of them are known to anyone who has studied Brathwaite's work: some of them are in danger of becoming stock images. But there are some others that stand out, and among these are some shots that feature Brathwaite in the company of other (often less well-known) individuals.

The circulation of stock photos of an individual does not in itself signify that the individual portrayed is himself a stock figure. It rather points to the fact that individuals or institutions that seek to present a visual image of writers like Brathwaite often resort to widely published images, opting for ease of access rather than visual innovation. This is also the case with the 2006 Griffin Trust for Excellence's YouTube video citation that introduces Brathwaite's reading of an excerpt from *Born to Slow Horses* at the location <http://www.youtube.com/watch?v=PbHQAK2J7NA>. This Web video is stifled by the lack of creative application. It appears hurriedly put together, drawing from stock images and hardly showing any attempt to convey the level of excellence that defines the stature of the poet and that of the Trust. But perhaps the choice of platform is partly responsible for the type of presentation produced there. Part of YouTube's identity is its nonsophistication. The vast majority of videos there are amateur in quality and production. No offence is therefore intended to their subject when some videos appear amateur: indeed, the amateur video aesthetic has infiltrated aspects of Western pop culture, especially film, music videos, and – most significantly in the post-2000 period – reality television. YouTube is therefore a product of the ethos of informality that has saturated Western pop culture at the beginning of the twenty-first century.

The Brathwaite video itself is not tacky or poor quality; it is acceptable YouTube fare. Up to May 2008 it had received more than 2393 views and one text comment that says: 'Very thought-provoking'. The choice of YouTube for staging this event on the occasion of Brathwaite's winning the prestigious Griffin Poetry Prize actually works well, given Brathwaite's performance aura and his previous innovations (for example, his recording of his poetry to vinyl back in the 1960s, anticipating the expansion of this interface by dub poets during the audio-cassette craze of the 1970s and 1980s). This, his first YouTube feature performance, does not in itself appear to exceed what one knows about Brathwaite the performer. The presentation uses a single camera positioned to the front of the lectern from which he reads his poem. The shot is wide angled, capturing him above the knees. There are no close-up shots to alleviate the distance that the clip sets up between the poet and his audience, and the poet and the video-maker. The excerpt, which chronicles the personal responses of the poet to death in his family, therefore appears to exist more as a document for storage/archiving and less as a moment/event-specific production. It arguably therefore leaves the dramatic input to the poet whom it believes has the presence and expertise to convey this.

Given Brathwaite's interest in the computer and its capacity to convey the voice, it is surprising that much more of his work is not staged on the Internet. Yes, you can hear him reading at the University of Miami's exciting Caribbean Writers Workshop Archive and at other selected educational sites, but one feels that there are many more avenues that this poet can continue to explore – for after all, he has championed what he calls the 'post-modem style'.

If some visuals of Brathwaite online tend to compress his representation, writings about him on selected blogs have moved away from a concern with his poetry to a concern with his plight as he wrestles to save his home in Barbados at his dwelling called CowPasture. The ongoing blog discourse and activism about the government of his country's plan to acquire the poet's land for an airport road reconnects the reader to the hard issues in the actual life of the poet. It is ironic that a medium (computer) Brathwaite has referenced and imagined in his work for years has evolved to grant him his most effective space for rallying support. Due to the personal impact of his struggle to keep his home, the reader gets an even more vivid image of who the poet is, outside the cocoon of his poetry. You therefore begin to imagine the connections between his current state of psychological dislocation and the kind of disquiet that his early poetry presents as it deals with the placelessness of the African. This phenomenon of physical and cultural exile is sounded and resounded in the eternal question of *The Arrivants*: 'Where then is the Negro's home?'.

Bibliography

ACHEBE, Chinua. 'English and the African Writer', *Transition* 18 (1965): 27–30.

AMANUDDIN, Syed. 'Towards a View of Commonwealth Poetic Tradition', *Awakened Conscience*. Ed. C. D. Narasinghaiah.

ANOZIE, Sunday. 'Okigbo's "Heavensgate": A Study of Art as Ritual', *Ibadan*. 15 (1963): 11–13.

—. 'A Structural Approach to Okigbo's "Distances"', *Conch*. 1, 1 (1969): 19–29.

—. 'Poetry and Empirical Logic: A Correspondence Theory of Truth in Okigbo's "Laments"', *Conch*. 2, 1 (1970): 54–65.

—. *Christopher Okigbo; Creative Rhetoric*. London: Evans Brothers Limited, 1972.

ARNOLD, Matthew. 'Stanzas in Memory of the Author of "Obermann"', *Criticism and the Nineteenth Century*. Ed. G. Tillotson.

AWOONOR, Kofi. 'Lament', *Short African Plays*. Ed. C. Pieterse. London: Heinemann, 1972.

AZUONYE, Nnorom. 'My e-conversation with Obi Nwakanma', Dec. 2002. <www.sentinelpoetry.org.uk/NnoromAzuonye_MyeConversationsWithObiNwakanma>. Accessed 7 Oct., 2008.

BABALOLA, S. A. 'The Characteristic Features of Outer Form in Yoruba Ijala Chants', *Odu*, 1, 1 – 2. (1964–5): 33–77.

BAUGH, Edward, ed. *Critics on Caribbean Literature*. London: George Alien & Unwin, 1978.

—.'Edward Brathwaite as Critic', *Critical Approaches to West Indian Literature*. Ed. Roberta Knowles and Erika Smilowitz. Virgin Islands: Humanities Division, 1981.

BEBEY, Francis. *African Music; A People's Art*. New York: Lawrence Hill and Co., 1975.

BEIER, Ulli. 'Three Mbari Poets', *Black Orpheus*, 12 (1962): 40–49.
—. *Python; Ibo Poetry*. Port Moresby: Papua Pocket Poets, 1967.
—. *African Poetry*. London: Cambridge University Press, 1971.
—. Review of Heavensgate in 'Three Mbari Poets', *Critical Perspectives on Christopher Okigbo*. Ed. Donatus Nwoga. 43–44.
BEST, Curwen. *Roots to Popular Culture*. Basingstoke: Macmillan, 2001.
—. *Culture @ the Cutting Edge*. Kingston: University of the West Indies Press, 2004.
—. *The Politics of Caribbean Cyberculture*. New York: Palgrave, 2008.
BLUNT, Anthony. *French Art and Music Since 1500*. London: Methuen, 1974.
BRATHWAITE, Edward K. *Rights of Passage*. ARGO PLP 111011 (1969).
—. *Contemporary Poets of the English Language*. London: St James Press, 1970.
—. *Masks*. ARGO PLP 1183 (1972).
—. *Islands*. ARGO PLP 11844/5 (1973).
—. *The Arrivants: A New World Trilogy*. Oxford: Oxford University Press, 1973.
—. *Other Exiles*. London: Oxford University Press, 1975.
—. *Black and Blues*. La Habana: Casa de Las Americas, 1976.
—. *Mother Poem*. Oxford: Oxford University Press, 1977.
—. *Sun Poem*. Oxford: Oxford University Press, 1982.
—. *Third World Poems*. London: Longman, 1983.
—. *History of the Voice*. London: New Beacon Books, 1984.
—. *X/Self*. Oxford: Oxford University Press, 1987.
—. *The Arrivants*. SavacouNorth CD SA 001 (2001).
BROWN, Lalage. 'The Development of African Prose Writing in English: A Perspective', *Perspectives on African Literature*. Ed. Christopher Heywood. 33–48.
BROWN, Lloyd. *West Indian Poetry*. Boston: Twayne Publishers, 1978.

BURNETT, Paula. *Penguin Book of Caribbean Verse.* Harmondsworth: Penguin Books Limited, 1986.

CANTOR, Paul. *Creature and Creator.* Cambridge: Cambridge University Press, 1945.

CARRINGTON, Lawrence, ed. *Studies in Caribbean Language.* Cave Hill: UWI School of Education, 1983.

CHADWICK, H. M. *The Growth of Literature.* 3 vols. London: Cambridge, 1932–1940.

CHERNOFF, John. *African Rhythm and African Sensibility.* Chicago: University of Chicago Press, 1979.

CHINWEIZU, et al. *Towards The Decolonialization of African Literature.* Washington, D.C: Howard University Press, 1983.

CHINWEIZU. 'Prodigals Come Home', *Critical Perspectives on Christopher Okigbo.* Ed. Donatus Nwoga. 177–183.

—. *Voices from Twentieth-Century Africa.* London: Faber and Faber, 1988.

COLEMAN, James. *Nigeria; A Background of Nationalism.* Berkeley: University of California Press, 1971.

CORDWELL, J. 'Continuity and Change in African Cultures', *Artist and Audience.* Eds. Richard Priebe and Thomas Hale.

COURTHOPE, William. *A History of English Poetry.* Vol.6 New York: Macmillan, 1895.

CROWDER, Michael. *The Story of Nigeria.* London: Faber, 1978.

DATHORNE, O. R. *African Literature in the Twentieth Century.* London: Heinemann Educational Books, 1974.

—. *The Black Mind.* Minneapolis: University of Minnesota Press, 1974.

DÖHNE, J. L. *A Zulu-Kaffir Dictionary.* Capetown, 1857.

DREW, Elizabeth. *T S Eliot; The Design of his Poetry.* New York: Scribner's, 1949.

ECHERUO, Michael. 'The Dramatic Limits of Igbo Ritual', *Critical Perspectives on Nigerian Literatures*. Ed. Bernth Lindfors. 75–85.

EGUDU, Romanus et al. *Igbo Traditional Verse*. London: Heinemann, 1971.

EGUDU, Romanus. 'Okigbo's Distances: A Retreat from Christ to Idoto', *Critical Perspectives on Christopher Okigbo*. Ed. Donatus Nwoga. 153–166.

EKECHI, Felix. *Traditional Transformation in Eastern Nigeria*. Ohio: Kent State University Press, 1989.

EKWE-EKWE, Herbert. 'Christopher Okigbo and These Times', *Kwenu!: Our Culture Our Future*. 19 May 2004. <www.kwenu.com/publications/ekwe-ekwe/okigbo_times.htm>. Accessed 20 Nov. 2007.

ELIOT, T. S. *Selected Essays*. London: Faber, 1951.

FINNEGAN, Ruth. *Oral Literature in Africa*. Nairobi: Oxford University Press, 1970.

FRASER, Robert. *West African Poetry; A Critical History*. Cambridge: Cambridge University Press, 1986.

GÖRLACH, Manfred, ed. *Focus on the Caribbean,* Philadelphia: John Benjamin Publishing, 1986.

GUTHRIE, M. 'Some Developments in the Prehistory of the Bantu Languages', *Journal of African History* 3, 2 (1962): 273–282.

HARRIS, Wilson. *Tradition, the Writer and Society*. London: New Beacon, 1967.

HEYWOOD, Anne-Marie. 'The Ritual and the Plot: The Critic and Okigbo's *Labyrinths*', *Critical Perspectives on Christopher Okigbo*. Ed. Donatus Nwoga. 207–225.

HEYWOOD, Christopher. *Perspectives on African Literature*. London: Heinemann, 1971.

HO LUNG, Richard. 'Sinner. Fame Priest Raps on God and Culture', *Caribbean Contact*. 2, 9 Dec. (1974): 19.

Holy Bible, King James version. Tennessee: Crusade Bible Publishers Inc., 1977.

IKIDDEH, Ime. 'Iron, Thunder and Elephants: A Study of Okigbo's "Path of Thunder"', *Critical Perspectives on Christopher Okigbo*. Ed. Donatus Nwoga. 184–195.

IRELE, Abiola. 'The Criticism of Modern African Literature', *Perspectives on African Literature*. Ed. Christopher Heywood. 9–24.

IRVINE, Alex. 'Postcolonial Generations: Yeats and Okigbo', n.d <http://alexirvine.net/okigbo.pdf>. Accessed 21 July, 2007.

IZEVBAYE, Dan. 'From Reality to the Dream: The Poetry of Christopher Okigbo', *Critical Perspectives on Christopher Okigbo*. Ed. Donatus Nwoga. 300–327.

JAHN, Janheinz. *Neo-African Literature: A History of Black Writing*. New York: Grove Press, 1968.

JONES, E D. 'The Decolonization of African Literature', *Topaz*. 21 (1968): 18–20.

JOSEPHS, Kelly Baker. 'Versions of *X/Self*: Kamau Brathwaite's Caribbean Discourse', *Anthurium* 1, 1 Fall, 2003. <http://scholar.library.miami.edu/anthurium/volume_1/issue_1/josephs-versions.htm>. Accessed 30 July, 2007.

KELLMAN, Anthony. 'A Rich Plural Heritage as a Tool for Survival', A review of *X/Self* by Edward Kamau Brathwaite. *Callaloo*, 36 (Summer, 1988): 645–648.

KILLAM, G. D, ed. *African Writers on African Writing*. London: Heinemann Educational Books, 1973.

KING, Bruce. 'Nationalism, Internationalism, Periodisation and Commonwealth Literature', *The History and Historiography of Commonwealth Literature*. Ed. Dieter Riemenschneider. Tübingen: Gunter Narr, 1983. 10–18.

KNAPPERT, Jan. *Traditional Swahili Poetry*. Leiden: EJ Brill, 1967.

LAMBO, T. Adeoye. 'The Place of the Arts in the Emotional Life of the African', *A.M.S.A.C. Newsletter*, 17 January (1965): 1–6.

LAMMING, George. 'The Peasant Roots of the West Indian Novel', *Critics on Caribbean Literature*. Ed. Edward Baugh. 24–26.

LEACH, Edmund. *Culture and Communication*. London: Cambridge University Press, 1976.

LE PAGE, Robert. 'Dialect in West Indian Literature', *Critics on Caribbean Literature*. Ed. Edward Baugh. 123–129.

LINDFORS, Bernth, ed. *Dem-say: Interviews with Eight Nigerian Writers*. Austin: University of Texas at Austin, 1974.

—. ed. *Critical Perspectives on Nigerian Literatures*. Washington: Three Continents Press, 1976.

LONG, Edward. *The History of Jamaica*. London: For T Lowndes, 1774.

MCSWEENEY, Joyelle. 'Kamau Brathwaite, *Ancestors*'. *Octopus Magazine* Issue 5, 2001. <http://www.octopusmagazine.com/issue05/recovery_project/mcsweeney_on_brathwaite.htm>. Accessed 30 July, 2007.

MCWATT, Mark. 'The Two Faces of El Dorado: Contrasting Attitudes Towards History and Identity in West Indian Literature', *Proceedings of the IVth Annual Conference on West Indian Literature*. Ed. Mark McWatt. Barbados, UWI, Cave Hill, 1985. 33–47.

MÁRQUEZ, Gabriel García. *In Evil Hour*. London: Jonathan Cape, 1980.

MAZRUI, Ali. *The Trial of Christopher Okigbo*. London: Heinemann, 1971.

MOORE, Gerald. 'Vision and Fulfillment', *Critical Perspectives on Christopher Okigbo*. Ed. Donatus Nwoga. 274–287.

MURPHY, Rosalie. *Contemporary Poets of the English Language*. London: St James Press Ltd., 1970.

NARASINGHAIAH, C. D, ed. *Awakened Conscience*. Kowloon: Heinemann, 1978.

NGARA, Emmanuel. *Stylistic Criticism of the African Novel*. London: Heinemann, 1982.

NGUGI wa Thiong'o. *Homecoming*. London: Heinemann, 1972.

—. Prefatory Notes to *The Colonial Legacy in Caribbean Literature* by Amon Saba Saakana. 9–11.

NKETIA, J. H. *The Music of Africa*. London: Victor Gallancz, 1975.

NKOSI, Louis. 'Interview with Christopher Okigbo', *Critical Perspectives on Christopher Okigbo*. Ed. Donatus Nwoga. 237–242.

NOSKE, Frits. *French Song from Berlioz to Duparc*. New York: Dover Publications, 1970.

NWACHUKWU, P. A. *Towards an Igbo Literary Standard*. London: Kegan Paul, 1983.

NWOGA, Donatus, ed. *Critical Perspectives on Christopher Okigbo*. Washington: Three Continents Press, 1984.

—.'Okigbo's "Limits": An Approach to Meaning', *Critical Perspectives on Christopher Okigbo*. Ed. Donatus Nwoga. 95–104.

OKAFOR, Dubem. *The Dance of Death: Nigerian History and Christopher Okigbo's Poetry*. Trenton: Africa World Press, 1998.

OKARA, Gabriel. *The Voice*. London: Heinemann Educational Books, 1964.

OKIGBO, Christopher. *Labyrinths*. London: Heinemann Educational Books, 1971.

OKUNOYE, Oyeniyi. 'Captives of Empire: Early Ibadan Poets and Poetry', *African Study Monograph*, 19, 3 (Nov., 1998): 161–170.

OSADEBAY, Dennis. *Africa Sings*. Ilfracombe: Stockwell, 1952.

PARRINDER, Geoffrey. *African Mythology*. London: Paul Hamlyn, 1967.

POLLARD, Charles, W. *New World Modernisms*. Charlottesville: University of Virginia Press, 2004.

PRIEBE, Richard, and Thomas Hale, eds. *Artist and Audience*. Washington: Three Continents Press, 1979.

RECKIN, Ann. 'Tidalectic Lectures: Kamau Brathwaite's Prose/Poetry as Sound-Space', *Anthurium* 1, 1 fall 2003. <http://anthurium.miami.edu/volume_1/issue_1/reckin-tidalectic.htm>. Accessed 30 Sept., 2007.

RIEMENSCHNEIDER, Dieter, ed. *The History and Historiography of Commonwealth Literature*. Tübingen: Gunter Narr, 1983.

RISDEN, Winifred. 'Review of "Masks" by Edward Brathwaite', *Caribbean Quarterly*, 14, 1 & 2, March–June (1968): 145–147.

ROHLEHR, Gordon. *Pathfinder: Black Awakening in The Arrivants*. Tunapuna: Gordon Rohlehr, 1981.

ROSCOE, Adrian. *Uhuru's Fire*. London: Cambridge University Press, 1977.

SAAKANA, Amon Saba. *The Colonial Legacy in Caribbean Literature*. London: Karnak House, 1987.

SCHAFER, Jürgen. 'Nation or Language', *The History and Historiography of Commonwealth Literature*. Ed. Dieter Riemenschneider. 3–9.

SELVON, Samuel. *Ways of Sunlight*. Washington: Three Continents Press, 1957.

SENGHOR, Léopold. *La Parole Chez Paul Claudel et Chez Les Négro-Africains*. Dakar: Les Nouvelles Editions Africaines, 1973.

SMEED, J. *Faust In Literature*. London: Oxford University Press, 1975.

ST. JOHN, Bruce. *Bumbatuk: Poems in Barbadian Dialect*. Bridgetown: Cedar Press, 1982.

SULE, Emmanuel. 'Literacy Language and Recent Nigerian Fiction', 29 Nov. 2005. <www.africanwriter.com/articles188/1>. Accessed 10 June, 2008.

SUTTON, Walter. *Ezra Pound, A Collection of Critical Essays*. Englewood Cliffs: Prentice-Hall, Inc., 1963.

TIFFIN, Helen. 'Commonwealth Literature: Comparison and Judgment', *History and Historiography*. Ed. Dieter Riemenschneider. 19–35.

TILLOTSON, Geoffrey, ed. *Criticism and the Nineteenth Century*. London: Athlone Press, 1951.

TORRES-SAILLANT, Silvio. 'The Trials of Authenticity in Kamau Brathwaite', *World Literature Today*, 68, Autumn, (1994): 697–707.

TUTUOLA, Amos. *The Palm-Wine Drinkard*. London: Faber and Faber, 1952.

UCHENDU, Victor. *The Igbo of Southeast Nigeria*. Austin: Holt, Rinehart & Winston Inc., 1965.

UDECHUKWU, Obiora. 'Aesthetics and the Mythic Imagination', *Critical Perspectives on Christopher Okigbo*. Ed. Donatus Nwoga. 78–85.

UDOEYOP, Nyong. 'Okigbo: A Branch of Giant Fennel', *Critical Perspectives on Christopher Okiqbo*. Ed. Donatus Nwoga. 167–176.

USHIE, Joe. 'Phases in Nigerian Poetry in English'. 21 July 2007. <http://64.233.169.104/search?q=cache:wuPEHw4FYm8J:www.africaresearch.org/Papers/N05/Ush1.pdf+okigbo+path+of+thunder+and+earlier+poetry&hl=en&ct=clnk&cd=18>. Accessed 21 July, 2007.

WALCOTT, Derek. 'What the Twilight Says: An Overture', *Dream on Monkey Mountain and Other Plays*. New York: Farrar, Strauss & Giroux, 1970.

WARNER-LEWIS, Maureen. *Notes to Masks*. Benin city: Ethiope Publishing, 1977.

WATERHOUSE, Keith. *New Statesman*. LX 17 September (I960).

WHITELEY, W. *Swahili, The Rise of a National Language*. London: Methuen, 1969.

WHITMAN, Walt. *The Portable Walt Whitman*. Harmondsworth: Penguin, 1977.

WILLIAMS, Emily Allen. *The Critical Response to Kamau Brathwaite*. Westport: Greenwood, 2004.

WOOD, Molara. 'Molara Wood: The Writings of a General Wordsbody', April 2006. <http://molarawood.blogspot.com/2006/04/mother-idoto-for-christopher-okigbo.html>. Accessed 16 May, 2008.

WRIGHT, Edgar. 'African Literature: Problems of Criticism', *Journal of Commonwealth Literature*, 2, Dec. (1966): 103–112.

——. ed. *Critical Evaluation of African Literature*. London: Heinemann Educational Books, 1973.

YESUFU, A.R. 'Ritual and the Quest for Selfhood in Okigbo's *Labyrinths* and Brathwaite's *Masks*', *NeoHelicon*. 28, 1 (2001): 236–245.

YOUNG, Peter. 'Tradition, Language and the Reintegration of Identity in West African Literature in English', *Critical Evaluation of African Literature*. Ed. Edgar Wright. 23–50.

Credits

A version of Chapter three 'Creative Pathways in Selected Poetry by Kamau Brathwaite and Christopher Okigbo' appeared in *Atlantic Critical Review* vol. 6. 4. (2007). 36–50.

A version of Chapter six 'Something Like A Mass: Ritual and Ceremony in Okigbo's "Heavensgate" and "Limits"' appeared in *The Atlantic Literary Review* Vol. 6 .3 (2006) 49–62.

A version of Chapter nine 'Return of the Town Crier? Okigbo's "Path of Thunder" and *Labyrinths*' appeared in *West Africa Review: Bioden Jeyifo and Africa*. Issue 11 (2007) http://www.westafricareview.com/issue11/toc11.htm .

Index